Railways and Industry
on the
BRECON & MERTHYR

SOUTH WALES VALLEYS

Railways and Industry on the BRECON & MERTHYR

Bargoed to Pontsticill Jct.
Pant to Dowlais Central

JOHN HODGE and RAY CASTON

PEN & SWORD
TRANSPORT

AN IMPRINT OF PEN & SWORD BOOKS LTD.
YORKSHIRE ~ PHILADELPHIA

Front Cover Caption: The more modern Pannier Tanks of the 8750 Class were much employed on the line in the final years of service with Ebbw Junction's 46XX series No. 4679 in charge of the 11.15am Newport to Brecon in the sunshine of 22nd December 1962 seen running over the level crossing and passing the small signal box at Dowlais Top, a week before the closure of the service on the 29th, when there was snow on the ground. (Gerald T. Robinson)

Back Cover Top Caption: North of Fochriw Ebbw Junction's 7736 makes a fine shot in the mountainous landscape as it climbs towards Dowlais Top with the 11.15am Newport to Brecon on 31st August 1957. R.O. (R.O.Tuck/Rail Archive Stephenson)

Back Cover Bottom Caption: Bargoed North Junction in the late 1950s/early 1960s as a 2251 Class 0-6-0 arrives with the 2.15pm Brecon to Newport. (Ken Mumford Presentations)

First published in Great Britain in 2022 by
Pen and Sword Transport
An imprint of
Pen & Sword Books Ltd.
Yorkshire - Philadelphia

Copyright © John Hodge and Ray Caston, 2022

ISBN 978 1 39907 076 8

The right of John Hodge and Ray Caston to be identified as authors of this work has been asserted by them in accordance with the Copyright, Designs and Patents Act 1988.

A CIP catalogue record for this book is available from the British Library.

Typeset in Palatino 11/13 by SJmagic DESIGN SERVICES, India.

Printed and bound by Printworks Global Ltd, London/Hong Kong.

Pen & Sword Books Ltd incorporates the imprints of Pen & Sword Books Archaeology, Atlas, Aviation, Battleground, Discovery, Family History, History, Maritime, Military, Naval, Politics, Railways, Select, Transport, True Crime, Fiction, Frontline Books, Leo Cooper, Praetorian Press, Seaforth Publishing, Wharncliffe and White Owl.

For a complete list of Pen & Sword titles please contact

PEN & SWORD BOOKS LIMITED
47 Church Street, Barnsley, South Yorkshire, S70 2AS, England
E-mail: enquiries@pen-and-sword.co.uk
Website: www.pen-and-sword.co.uk

or

PEN AND SWORD BOOKS
1950 Lawrence Rd, Havertown, PA 19083, USA
E-mail: Uspen-and-sword@casematepublishers.com
Website: www.penandswordbooks.com

CONTENTS

DEDICATION

This book is dedicated to two of the photographers whose material helps to make up this account, namely R.O. Tuck and Sid Rickard. I (John Hodge) first met Bob Tuck in 1954 at the west end of Platforms 1 and 2 at Cardiff General as we were both awaiting the 3.50pm Whitland to Kensington Milk. At that time, I was mastering the engine diagrams working through Cardiff and gave him the working for that Swindon diagram. We quickly became friends, though he was much older than I, in his early forties whereas I was at Barry Grammar School, aged 16, just a little older than Bob's son Philip, whom I also soon got to know, and his daughter Margaret. We would go on the Sunday trips around Swindon Works, making a mad-dash car drive from Cardiff to Swindon, up over Birdlip, Glos., in the days before the M4 and Severn Bridge. Bob was in charge of the Post Office Training School at Penarth and politically was a strong member of the Co-Operative Movement, his full name being Robert Owen Tuck, after its founder. We remained friends until I moved away from South Wales in 1970 and only saw each other on very rare occasions afterwards. He lived to the ripe old age of 91, still photographing into his late eighties, and still interested to the end in the railway's goings-on.

Sid Rickard was a close friend of Bob's, but I only ever met him once when we all went to Swansea for the final day of the Mumbles Trams, and a pretty grotty wet day it was, certainly not lending itself to good photography. There was a bit of a divergence of interest between Sid and me; he was more interested in the Valleys and local lines, whereas I was all for the main line. He used to exhort me to 'get up the Valleys while they are still there', and of course he was right, as vast swathes of them are now history. Fortunately, he photographed the Valleys in detail and his collection is now held by Keith Jones and Malcolm James as the J&J Collection and is very well used in my books on South Wales. Sid moved from Cardiff to Glasgow in the 1970s, and died in the 1980s, but he is still well remembered as the best photographer of the South Wales Valleys with Michael Hale.

ACKNOWLEDGEMENTS

Our thanks go to R.A. Cooke for use of his *Track Layout Diagrams* and *Gazetteer of the Coal Mines of South Wales & Monmouthshire* for information on the collieries north of Bargoed, to Keith Jones of Mountain Ash and Malcolm James of Rogerstone for the use of the many Sid Rickard photographs now held in their J&J Collection. Thanks also to Ian Reece for help with editing and Michael Roach, Jeff Stone and Garth Tilt for the use of their photos from their visits to the line and to Ken Mumford for material from his B&M presentation.

Every effort has been made to identify the copyright holder for photographs and other material used. Where this has not been possible, please contact john_hodge@ tiscali.co.uk by email if there is a need to rectify the position.

AUTHORS' NOTE

Many Welsh place names were spelt in two or more ways especially during the nineteenth century, e.g. Pantywaen or Pantywaun or Pant-y-Waun. We have used either/all the different spellings in this book so the reader has a flavour of the diversity. This also applied to people's names e.g. Ifor or Ivor Works at Dowlais.

Dowlais based TV 04 333 with a service to Pant or Pontsticill awaiting departure on 12 August 1939. (F.K. Davies)

INTRODUCTION

The section of the Brecon & Merthyr (B&M) between Bargoed and Pontsticill saw a marked change in nature and scenery, compared with the railway above Pontsticill, and below Bargoed which are dealt with in separate volumes. The line was built in a southerly direction, the section above Pontsticill being one of dramatic yet beautiful scenery as the Brecon Beacons rolled down to the valley floor and opened out to large reservoirs, the waters from which went to service the South Wales Valleys. The original main intention of the line planners south of Pontsticill was to access the ironworks town of Dowlais with a line from Pant, then a main line, and to access the other major ironworks town of Merthyr, then the most important town in Wales, due to its several ironworks, both towns' works giving them worldwide acclaim and standing. The B&M would continue its southern progress by building its line from Pant down to meet with the Rhymney Railway pushing north from Bargoed into the industrial area surrounding Dowlais from its more southerly standpoint, and south of Dowlais Top meeting with the Pantywaun coalfield, which supplied Dowlais ironworks, then reaching Fochriw and the collieries below in the valley which both fed their coal to Dowlais and more generally into the South Wales, foreign and other markets. The closure of Dowlais Works for iron and steel production caused the abandonment of the Pantywaun coalfield and in the course of time the other collieries in the area of Fochriw and to the south. This left the area with fewer, but larger, collieries into the 1950s north of Bargoed, which were finally reduced to just Ogilvie and Groesfaen, and finally just to Ogilvie.

North of Bargoed, the southbound B&M line down to Deri Junction was mostly single line with passing loops at stations, but the original Rhymney Railway line south of Deri Jct. was double to accommodate coal trains to and from Groesfaen, Fochriw, Pantywaun and later Ogilvie collieries. The line north of this industrial complex became largely single with passing loops until Pontsticill Junction was reached, and then the other junction at Talyllyn before the outskirts of Brecon were reached at the original station Watton where the engine shed and traffic sidings were situated. Between Pant and Bargoed in the 1950s, the line catered for three passenger services, the basic trains to and from Brecon, the Dowlais Central to Bargoed, mostly workmen's, trains which were provided for the miners at Ogilvie, Groesfaen and Bargoed collieries, and also reciprocally, though mostly in the past, for workers at Dowlais Ironworks, and a service started by the GW to and from Dowlais Top, mostly to Bargoed but with a few trains working through to Cardiff and beyond. A bus connection at Dowlais Top afforded a service into and from Merthyr itself. Beyond Pant, the line from Merthyr rose gradually on the left to the level of a main line, affording the lovely view of the south end of the Taf Fechan Reservoir with the three features coming to level at Pontsticill Junction station.

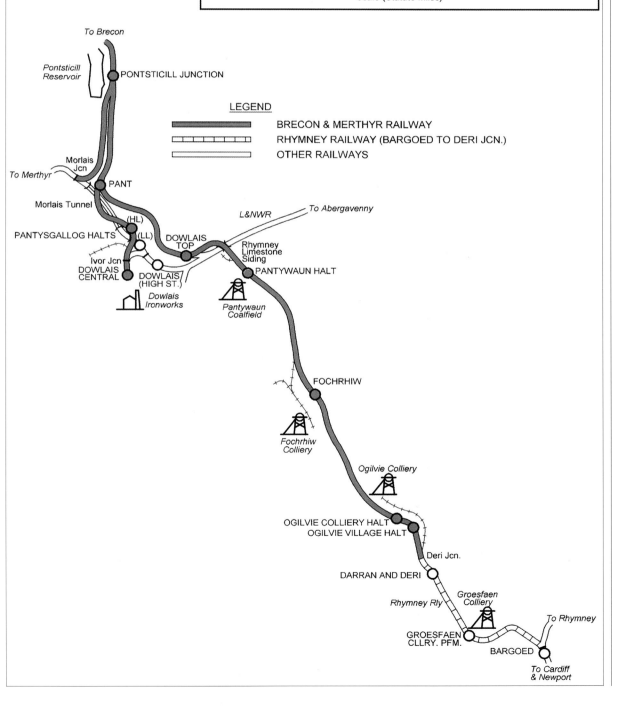

**BRECON & MERTHYR RAILWAY
(BARGOED TO PONTSTICILL JCN)**

Showing Collieries and Works

Richard Harman - January 2022

0   ½   1
Scale (Statute Miles)

Map of the B&M line between Brecon and Bargoed, including the branches from Pant to Dowlais Central (Lloyd Street) and Pontsticill to Merthyr.
(Richard Harman)

CHAPTER 1

SERVICES AFTER THE GROUPING BASED ON 1924 SERVICE TIMETABLE

Following the Grouping of 1922/23, when all former B&M operations were taken over by the GWR, the Service Timetable for 1924 sets out the services as they were to operate for many years afterwards. The final Newport to Brecon through services in the 1950s and '60s show a marked similarity to those in 1924. The main change was on the goods services. In the 1920s while the Pantywaen coalfield was still operative to serve the Dowlais Ironworks, the GWR used the location as a marshalling point for freight traffic generally in that part of the B&M. When Dowlais ceased production of iron and steel in 1936, all the local supplying collieries, many of which were small units, closed down and the former Pantywaen coalfield

disappeared, some units being included in the future Cwmbargoed Opencast development. The main flow of general freight over the B&M to and from Brecon had been via Pantywaen and its closure saw the introduction of a through service between Bassaleg and Brecon and reverse, which had previously operated to and from Pantywaen. In B&M days, Talyllyn Jct. either had a shunting engine based there or one provided from Brecon to interchange freight traffic between the B&M and Mid-Wales services. In later GWR and BR days, shunting was variously carried out by the train engines of the Brecon to Bassaleg, Merthyr to Talyllyn or Brecon and Brecon to Moat Lane freight services, and this could also be encompassed at Pontsticill.

Passenger Services
Newport-Brecon. Four services operated in each direction, as follows:-

Dep NPT	Bargoed	Pontsticill	Arr, BCN
8.15am	9.15-9.19am	9.54-9.59am	11.00am
10.55am	11.56-12.00	12.35-12.40pm	1.40pm
2.45pm	3.44-3.48pm	4.23-4.30pm	5.30pm
6.50pm	7.49-7.53pm	8.28-8.40pm	9.31pm

Brecon-Newport

Dep. BCN	Pontsticill	Bargoed	Arr. NPT.
7.35am	8.35-8.40am	9.11-9.14am	10.20am
12noon	1.2-1.8pm	1.39-1.40pm	2.45pm
2.5pm	3.12-3.16pm	3.48-3.51pm	4.53pm
6.8pm	7.5-7.12pm	7.43-7.46pm	8.47pm

As can be seen, it was roughly an hour's travelling time between Newport to Bargoed and Pontsticill and Brecon.

Through services

Northbound
10.20am Cardiff Parade to Pontsticill MSO. Bargoed 11.9-11.14am Pontsticill arr. 11.50am
11.20am Merthyr to Brecon MSX Pontsticill 11.46-11.55am Brecon arr. 12.50pm
9.40am Treherbert-Aberystwyth MSO Pont. 11.53-11.59am Talyllyn No.3 12.33pass
10.45am Barry-Llandrindod Wells MSO Pont 1.2-1.7pm Talyllyn No.3 1.44pm
8.25pm Pontsticill-Talyllyn ECS ThSO arr, 9.5pm.
(NB Talyllyn No. 3 was the future Talyllyn East Jct.)

Southbound
12.40pm Pontsticill Jct. to Cardiff Parade SO
2.45pm FO Brecon to Merthyr Pont. 3.41-3.42pm
12.20pm Aberystwyth to Treherbert MSO Pont. 5.8-5.12pm Merthyr 5.34-5.40pm
4.45pm Brecon to Merthyr Pont. 5.47-5.50pm Merthyr arr. 6.13pm
4.10pm Llandrindod Wells-Barry MSO Tal.No.3 5.32pm pass Pont. 6.21-6.24pm.

Merthyr 6.46-6.55pm
9.25pm Talyllyn to Merthyr ThSO Pont. 10.4-10.6pm Merthyr arr.10.29pm

Dowlais Central-Pant & Pontsticill

Dow.Dep.	Pant	Pontsticill
6.30am	6.35am	6.38am Wkmen
8.25am	8.30am	-
9.35am	9.40am	-
11.35am	11.40am	-
12.15pm	12.20pm	12.24pm
3.10pm FX	3.15pm	-
3.10pm FO	3.15pm	3.20
4.5pm	4.10pm	-
5.0pm MSO	5.5pm	-
7.0pm	7.5pm	-
8.10pm	8.15pm	-

Pontsticill	Pant	Dow. Arr.
-	8.51am TFX	8.56am
8.47am	8.51am TFO	8.56am
-	10.0am	10.5am
-	11.55am MSO	12noon
12.45pm Wkmen SO	-	12.54pm
	1.14pm	1.19pm
-	3.30pm FX	3.35pm
3.47pm FO	3.51pm	3.56pm
-	4.30pm	4.35pm
5.21pm Wkmen SX	-	5.30pm
-	5.40pm MSO	5.45pm
-	7.25pm	7.30pm
-	8.30pm	8.35pm

Through Services

Southbound
5.50am Dowlais Central to Dowlais Top Workmen & Passrs
2.40pm Ogilvie Colliery to Fleur de Lis (Serves Groesfaen) Workmen.
5.40pm Dowlais Top to Bargoed arr. 6.1pm MSX
5.30pm Pontsticill to Bargoed arr. 6.1pm MSO
8.55pm Fochriw to Bargoed arr. 9.7pm
9.15pm Dowlais Central to Fleur de Lis SO Pant 9.20-9.27pm

Northbound
6.18am Bargoed to Ogilvie Colliery PD Workmen
4.40pm Bargoed to Dowlais Top MSX arr. 5.4pm / to Pontsticill MSO arr. 5.16pm
8.30pm Bargoed to Fochriw arr. 8.45pm.
9.50pm Rhymney to Ogilvie Workmen Bargoed 1010-10.18pm
10.15pm Fleur de Lis-Dowlais Central SO 11.5pm

Coach Working for Newport to Brecon Services 1924
Set No. 55 *@ 7.35am Brecon to Newport ** 10.55am Newport to Brecon
        *2.5pm Brecon to Newport   *6.50pm Newport to Brecon
Formation: Brake Third, Third, Compo, Compo, Third, Van All 4 wheeled Stock
Notes * Extra Third SO ** Stores Van Swindon to Oswestry MO off 5.40am ex-Glos.
@ Empty Stores Van Brecon to Swindon ThO Connect 12.15pm Cardiff Parcels.
Set No. 56 9.55am Rhymney B&M to Newport 12.25pm Newport to Pontypool Road
1.10pm Pontypool Road to Newport
* 2.45pm Newport to Brecon * 6.8pm Brecon to Newport
Formation: Van Third, Third, Compo, Third, Van All 4 wheeled Stock
Notes * Extra Third SO
Set No. 58 * 8.15am Newport to Brecon * 12noon Brecon to Newport
* 3.40pm Newport to Rhymney B&M
Formation: Van Third, Third, Compo, Compo, Third, Van All 4 wheeled Stock.
Notes * Extra Third SO

Working of Swindon to Central Wales Stores Van

Day	Location	Arr.	Dep.
Mon.	Swindon		4.5am
	Gloucester	5.6am	5.40am
	Newport	7.10am	10.55am
	Talyllyn Jct.	1.18pm	1.35pm
	Moat Lane Jct.	3.35pm	4.54pm
	Oswestry	6.48pm	
Tues.	Oswestry		11.5am
	Machynlleth	1.44pm	2.40pm
	Barmouth	3.12pm	4.0pm
	Ruabon	6.8pm	8.5pm
	Oswestry	8.44pm	
Wed.	Oswestry		11.5am
	Moat Lane Jct.	12.47pm	2.50pm
	Brecon	5.12pm	
Thurs.	Brecon		7.35am
	Newport	10.20am	12.15pm
	Swindon	3.26pm	
Fri/Sat.	Loading at Swindon		

Goods Working (Based on 1924 Service TT)
Pantywaen Northbound
7.5am Bargoed J.Jct. to Pontsticill arr. 9.50am Pantywaen 7.49-8.35am
6.40am Bassaleg to Pantywaen arr. 9.59am. FldeLis 7.32-8.30am Bargoed 8.41-9am

11.20am Aberbargoed Jct. to Pantywaen arr.12.51pm
1.7pm Pantywaen to Brecon arr. 4.30pm Pontsticill 1.39-1.45pm
4.45pm Fleur de Lis Sdgs-Pantywaen arr. 6.10pm

Southbound
10.35am EBV Pantywaen to Aberbargoed Jct.
9.0am Brecon to Pantywaen arr. 12.33pm Pontsticill 11.35-12.0pm
1.50pm Pantywaen to Fleur de Lis Sdgs.
7.30pm Pantywaen to Fleur de Lis Sdgs. 9.18pm

Merthyr to Brecon Northbound
5am Merthyr to Talyllyn arr.7.45am Pontsticill 6.12-6.23am
9.10am Merthyr to Brecon arr. 12.40pm Pontsticill 10.50-11.5am
3.15pm Pontsticill to Brecon MSX arr. 5.55pm
4.15pm Pontsticill to Brecon MSO arr. 6.50pm
3.40pm Merthyr to Talyllyn arr. 6.50pm
7.5pm Merthyr to Brecon arr. 10.45pm ThSX 11.20pm ThSO

Southbound
5am Brecon to Merthyr Pontsticill 6.45-7am
8.45am Talyllyn to Merthyr Pontsticill 10.30-11am
12.40pm Talyllyn to Pontsticill MSX (11.40am LE Bcn-Tal)
1.45pm Talyllyn to Pontsticill MSO arr. 3.45pm (12.55pm LE Bcn-Tal.)
2.55pm Brecon to Merthyr Pontsticill 4.50-5.35pm
3.40pm Brecon to Merthyr Livestock Class E Pontsticill 5.25-5.55pm
7.30pm Talyllyn-Merthyr Pontsticill 9.20-9.50pm
All services were run as Class K except where shown

1950s Services Based on Summer Service 1958
Passenger
Following the withdrawal of public passenger services between Pant and
Dowlais Central on 28 June 1952, workmen's miners' services between Dowlais
Central and Ogilvie/Groesfaen collieries, which continued on to Bargoed for
operational purposes, continued to run and it is said that use was made of these
services by the public also. The workmen's services involved were, as at Summer
service 1958:-

Southbound
5.2am Dowlais Central to Bargoed arr. 5.57am
12.58pm Dowlais Central to Bargoed arr. 1.46pm
3.5pm ECS Dowlais central to Bargoed arr. 3.43pm
9.20pm Dowlais Central to Bargoed arr. 10.14pm SX

Northbound
6.40am Bargoed to Dowlais central arr. 7.34am
1.34pm Bargoed to Dowlais Central SO arr. 2.30pm
1.38pm Bargoed to Ogilvie Colliery arr. 2.5pm SX
2.39pm Bargoed to Dowlais Central arr. 3.28pm SX
10.35pm Bargoed to Dowlais central arr. 11.30pm

The public passenger service as at Summer 1958 were:

Southbound
6.35am Fochriw to Penarth DMU Bargoed 6.51-6.58am
7.35am Brecon to Newport Pontsticill 8.27-8.30am Bargoed 8.59-9.1am
12.47pm Dowlais Top to Cardiff Queen Street SO
12.15pm Brecon to Newport Pontsticill 1.14-1.16pm Bargoed 1.52-1.57pm
2.0pm Brecon to Newport Pontsticill 3.1-3.3pm Bargoed 3.36-3.37pm
5.30pm Dowlais Top to Bargoed arr.5.51pm
6.15pm SO Brecon to Newport Pontsticill 7.14-7.17pm Bargoed 7.49-7.51pm
8.30pm Brecon to Maesycwmmer SO Pont. 9.23-9.26pm Bargoed 9.59-10pm

Northbound
5.12am Ystrad Mynach to Fochriw arr. 6.9am DMU
8.3am Newport to Brecon Bargoed 9.0-9.9am Pontsticill 9.50-9.59am
11.35am Bargoed to Dowlais Top SO arr. 12.6pm DMU
11.15am Newport to Brecon Bargoed 12.11-12.16pm Pontsticill 12.54-12.56pm
3.0pm Newport to Brecon SO Bargoed 3.55-4.1pm Pontsticll 4.44-4.46pm
6.50pm Pant-Brecon SO Pontsticill 6.54-6.55pm
6.55pm Newport to Brecon Bargoed 7.50-7.55pm, Pontsticill 8.36-8.37pm

The existence of late Saturday evening trains probably stemmed from a GWR desire to cater for the cinema and dance market which was strong on Saturday evenings. The trains were however costly to run with only one round trip for the crew and often entailed ECS running. They tended to become victims of cost-cutting exercises in the 1960s.

Freight services based on 1959 Working Timetable

By this date, freight trains from Hereford (apart from the ammonia trains to Dowlais Central) only worked to three Cocks Jct., where traffic was exchanged with the Mid-Wales line workings to Brecon.

Northbound
7am Merthyr to Brecon arr. 9.48am Pontsticill 7.34-7.40am
9.20am Brecon to Builth Wells arr. 12.25pm
7.5am Bassaleg to Brecon arr. 2.45pm Pontsticill 11.45-11.55am
3.35pm Merthyr to Talyllyn Jct. Arr. 6.10pm Pontsticill 4.19-5pm
5pm Dowlais Central to Hereford (Ammonia to Billingham)
Pontsticill 5.20-5.20pm Talyllyn East Jct. pass 6.46pm

Southbound
7.15am Brecon to Bassaleg arr. 3.5pm Pontsticill 10.30-10.40am
10.50am Brecon to Merthyr Pontsticill 12.27-12.47pm
12.15pm Hereford to Dowlais Central
    arr. 4.17pm Talyllyn East Jct.
pass 2.29pm Pontsticill pass 3.41pm (Ammonia from Billingham)
10.15am Moat Lane to brecon arr. 8.15pm SX, 4.30pm SO
7pm Talyllyn Jct. to Merthyr Pontsticill 8.30-8.40pm

CHAPTER 2

LOCATION ANALYSIS

Bargoed

Bargoed was the meeting place in practice of the northern and southern sections of the Brecon & Merthyr Railway and was also a junction with the Rhymney Railway. In exact terms, the B&M built the line only down as far as Deri Junction (the later junction for Ogilvie Colliery) with the Rhymney building the line through to Bargoed North, where it joined the main Rhymney to Cardiff line of the Rhymney Railway, the new section being known as the Bargoed Rhymney. The B&M then built the line on from Bargoed South Junction to Bassaleg, which ran alongside Bargoed Colliery between Bargoed Station, Bargoed South Junction and Aberbargoed Junction.

A plan for 1875 shows that, until alterations to layout in 1900, the station consisted of two equal length platforms. In 1892, a goods yard and shed were installed on the east side of the Rhymney line just north of the junction between the two routes. Previously there was a single siding between the north end of the Down platform and the junction, with connections onto the running lines and this may well have afforded initial goods yard facilities. By 1900 there was a fully operational goods shed and yard in the position described which included the original siding. Also in 1900, the Up platform was made into an island, the additional platform enabling cross-platform connections between trains for the Bargoed-Rhymney line and Cardiff to Rhymney services; Up B&M trains used this new Platform 1 continuously, while all Down trains used the single Down Rhymney Platform 3. There were three signal boxs at Bargoed, Bargoed South Junction where the B&M joined the Rhymney, Bargoed North Junction in the triangle where the Bargoed Rhymney

diverged from the Rhymney, and Bargoed West at the north end of the loop on the Bargoed Rhymnney branch north of the station, and later controlling a new Down Refuge Siding and loop, with Up side sidings installed in 1901, used inter alia for stabling empty stock for the Bargoed-Pant/Dowlais trains.

This layout sufficed until the closure of the Brecon route at the end of 1962, following which only coal traffic and empties from and to Groesfaen and Ogilvie collieries remained, the Dowlais ammonia traffic being re-routed via Bargoed and the B&M/Vale of Neath in December 1962. The Down Refuge Siding between Bargoed West and North signal boxs was taken out of use in March 1964. The siding south of the station and the connection from the Up main to the west side of the island platform were both removed in January 1968, following singling of the former B&M line at Bargoed South in July 1965, with the signal box itself closing as part of the January 1968 works. The west side of the island platform remained as a siding, stop-blocked at the south end and accessed from Bargoed North. The Goods Shed and part of the yard were taken out of use in January 1969. Bargoed North Junction signal box closed in November 1970 and a new box was opened on the east side of the running lines, the main running line through the station having now been singled and been made bi-directional, the Down line and platform being retained in use though with the Up main retained as a loop mostly for coal empties to McLaren. The former Bargoed Rhymney line became known as the Ogilvie Branch, this colliery being the only source of traffic left on it. The sidings on the branch approaching

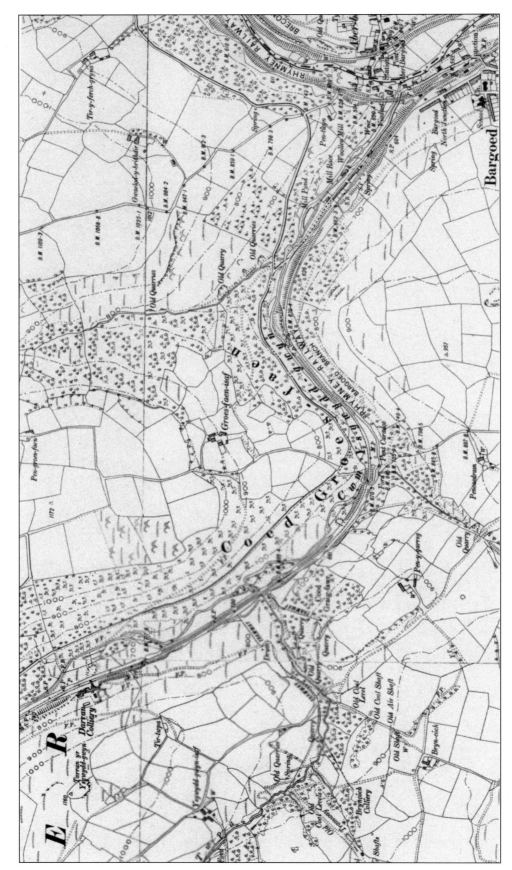

OS Map 1888-1913 of the Bargoed to Darran & Deri area. National Library of Scotland

Bargoed were taken out in September 1972 and the whole branch closed with the closure of Ogilvie Colliery in September 1978. Subsequently the Up platform has been brought back into use, the station functioning on an Up and Down platform basis, with many passenger trains terminating at and starting from Bargoed, while others run through to Rhymney.

Ebbw's 3638 provides the power for the 11.15am Newport to Brecon as it runs into Bargoed station, having run across from the B&M line. Bargoed Colliery forms the background on the left to this 2 May 1959 shot. (S. Rickard/ D.K. Jones J&J Collection)

Part of the island platform and footbridge seen from the platform used by services to Brecon as in 1962. (John Hodge)

The north end of the island platform with A Brecon bound train behind a 875X at Platform 1. (Ken Mumford Presentations)

Merthyr's 9616 pulls away from Bargoed with the 11.35am to Dowlais Top on 2 May 1959. (S. Rickard/ D.K. Jones J&J Collection)

Ebbw's newly acquired 2247 runs in off the branch on the former Rhymney Railway's lines through the down platform with the 2.10pm Brecon to Newport on 17 September 1962. (R.E. Toop)

In later years, the Brecon to Bassaleg Goods was often a light train as on 17 September 1962 when seen passing through Bargoed station with Ebbw's long term 2218 at the head. (R.E. Toop)

Brecon trains passing at Bargoed. 9644 with the 8.3am Newport to Brecon takes water while 3714 with the 7.35am ex-Brecon pass at the north end of Bargoed station on 4 November 1961. (Larry Fullwood/ Transport Treasury)

An unusual operation recorded at Bargoed, as a northbound freight service with a 56XX occupies the Brecon platform while the Brecon passenger service is accommodated at the northbound Rhymney platform. (Ken Mumford Presentations)

The 6.15pm Brecon to Newport takes water at the south end of the Down platform, headed by Ebbw's 3747 on 7 July 1962. (Malcolm James)

The 11.35am service to Dowlais Top was DMU operated on Saturdays with a return working at 12.47pm through to Cardiff Queen Street. Here the train is awaiting departure from Bargoed on 29 December 1962, the last day of service on the B&M. (John Hodge)

On the last day of service, 29 December 1962, 4627 takes water at the north end of Bargoed platform with the 11.15am Newport to Brecon. A notice on the tank says that there is no water available at Pant station on this final day. (R. Grainger/Ken Mumford Presentations)

The 7.35am and 2.10pm services from Brecon and the returning 11.15am and 6.55pm from Newport were worked by Brecon engines until Brecon lost its allocation in 1959, after which 2251 Class 0-6-0s and 57XX pannier tanks were provided by Ebbw Jct. and 465XX 2-6-0s by Oswestry. Here Brecon-based 46518 heads south from Bargoed. Following the removal of the turntable from Godfrey Road in Newport, tender engines off the inward Brecon service had to go out to the Maindee Triangle to turn. (David Lawrence/Hugh Davies Collection)

Passing Bargoed North SB 3706 pulls away from Bargoed with a Newport to Brecon three coach service on 27 April 1960. (R.K. Blencowe Collection)

The layout approaching Bargoed is well shown in this 1962 shot of a Dowlais Top to Bargoed train. (John Hodge)

Heading through Bargoed West with Bargoed Viaduct visible on the Rhymney line to the right, Rhymney's 5605 is enroute to Ogilvie Colliery with two BVs in April 1964. (A.E. Durrant/ D.K. Jones Collection)

Bargoed seen on 3 April 1965 from high ground above the viaduct which carries the line to Rhymney. The former Brecon line is now used only to service Groesfaen and Ogilvie Collieries. (Trevor Owen/ Colour Rail)

Bargoed North Junction in the late 1950s/early 1960s as a 2251 Class 0-6-0 arrives with the 2.15pm Brecon to Newport. (Ken Mumford Presentations)

Another view at Bargoed West, taken from the signal box, as 5651 heads a southbound train of coal from Ogilvie Colliery in April 1964. (A.E. Durrant/ D.K. Jones)

Bargoed West with Bargoed Viaduct on the line to Rhymney in the background as on 2 June 1968. (Garth Tilt)

Almost twenty years after the closure of the Brecon service and the Brecon track at Bargoed has been reduced to a siding, stop-blocked at the south end. A Rhymney Valley train departs south against the background of the huge Bargoed Colliery slagheap, probably the largest waste tip in the South Wales coalfield. This was landscaped and many trees planted to improve stability. (Ken Mumford Presentations)

Following the closure of the Brecon service, various replanning took place at Bargoed station. Platform 1, previously used by services to Brecon, has become a siding, stop-blocked at the south end and a train of coal is being accommodated there. A new signal box is being constructed at the north end of the down platform which will replace the former Bargoed North and the water tower has been removed to reflect the diesel age. (Ken Mumford Presentations)

With the Bargoed Viaduct in the background, 9675 leaves Bargoed with a train to Dowlais Central which will reverse at Pant.
(Ken Mumford Presentations)

Groesfaen

Just north of Bargoed West were the extensive sidings of Groesfaen Colliery, located on the east side of the line, with a sister pit originally located on land at Penygarreg farm. Sinking of the shaft by the Rhymney Iron Co. began in 1902 and the pit was opened in 1906 to a depth of 720 yards, the cost being £183,700. The produce was initially house coal produced from the Rhas Las seam but as the lower seams were reached (Red, Upper Four Feet, Seven Feet and Yard, in addition to the Rhas Las) steam coal was produced from 1924 onwards, production of house coal ceasing in 1923. A workmen's train from Pengam was introduced to a new platform at Groesfaen in February 1916. In April 1923, coal was raised from both Groesfaen and Penygarreg Collieries, the latter previously being the Upcast for Groesfaen. Both pits were closed for a while in 1925 due to a trade depression but were restarted again in October of that year.

An elevated view of Groesfaen Miners Platform on 11 June 1962. (Michael Hale/Great Western Trust)

Groesfaen Miners Platform as seen from a passing train in December 1962. (John Hodge)

During the late 1920s, Powell Duffryn acquired almost the whole of the share capital of the Rhymney Iron Co. which went into liquidation in the early 1930s when the pits came under the control of Powell Duffryn (PD). Production was extended to fireclay in 1937-8 with 140 men employed but following flooding of the area, this was abandoned.

By 1911 over 1,000 miners were employed, rising to over 1,400 by 1920 and almost 1,600 by 1931, after which it dropped back to 12-1,300 until the war and to about 1,000 until 1960 with a decline to around 800 in 1961-64 and 580 from 1965-67, the colliery closing in December 1968. Between 1954-7, production had been 220-257,000 tons, but by 1961 was down to 150,000,

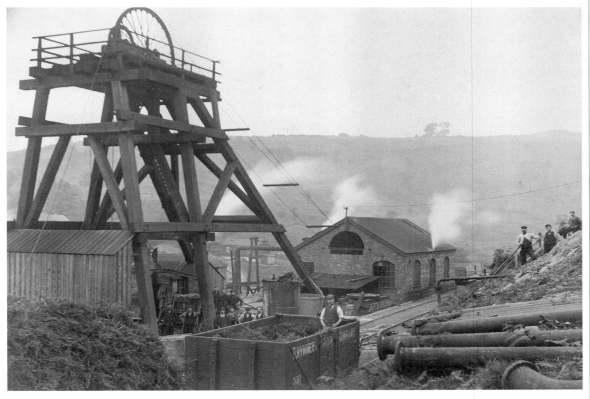

Views of Groesfaen Colliery. (R. Lawrence Collection)

Elevated views of Groesfaen Colliery, looking up the Darran Valley.
(Ken Mumford Presentations)

Groesfaen North
signal box on
8 August 1964.
(Garth Tilt)

Groesfaen South
on 8 August 1964.
(Garth tilt)

though in 1964/5 was back up to 207,000, equivalent to two loaded trains out per day.

Originally, west and south of Groesfaen were North and South Wingfield Collieries and the associated Mardy and Bryncoch pits. The Mardy Pit was opened in 1874 by Christopher James who formed the Mardy Colliery Co. It was 1880 before any coal was worked, though a siding was provided by the Rhymney Railway to serve the pit years earlier. Each colliery worked the Mynyddislwyn seam to produce house coal. In 1882, Mardy Colliery was purchased by Bevan & Price and renamed North Wingfield. Production was 34,800 tons in 1882, but the pit was stopped in 1884 and was not listed in 1885. It was back in production in 1886/7 with 12,300 and 28,100 tons respectively but was abandoned due to exhaustion in 1892 and sold off by auction.

South Wingfield was originally part of the Mardy and Wingfield group of collieries but from 1871 became a separate unit owned by Bevan & Price. In 1887, the lease was transferred to E. Beddoe, who also owned the Penygarreg Colliery, but the pit was abandoned in 1891 with his bankruptcy. The pit was in best production between 1878 (53,400 tons) and 1881 (85,100 tons) and between 1877 and 1885 produced between 500-600,000tons.

Bryncoch was part of the group of collieries opposite what later became Groesfaen Colliery but was owned from 1898-1903 by the Bryncoch Coal Co. It worked the Mynyddislwyn seam for house coal and was operated above ground as a tramway to sidings west of the Bargoed Rhymney line. It was a small undertaking with a maximum workforce of 44 men in 1900 and was in production between 1898 and April 1904.

Darran & Deri

Located at 20m.73ch. from Newport High Street station, on a 1 in 47 reverse gradient going north, Darran & Deri station was first known as Deri and then as Deri and Darran before the final combination was decided. It was a two-track station, the Rhymney Railway line becoming single at Deri Jct. (21m. 25ch.) where B&M metals were reached.

Darran & Deri station consisted of equal length Up and Down platforms. South of Darran & Deri station was the Darran Colliery in production between 1869 and 1923 and owned by the Rhymney Iron Co. Ltd., who took out a PSA with the Rhymney Railway in December 1868. Production reached a peak of almost 100,000 tons in 1880 and was often between 80-90,000 with a peak workforce

OS Map of the Darran & Deri area at the turn of the twentieth century. At this time, Ogilvie colliery had not been opened. (National Library of Scotland)

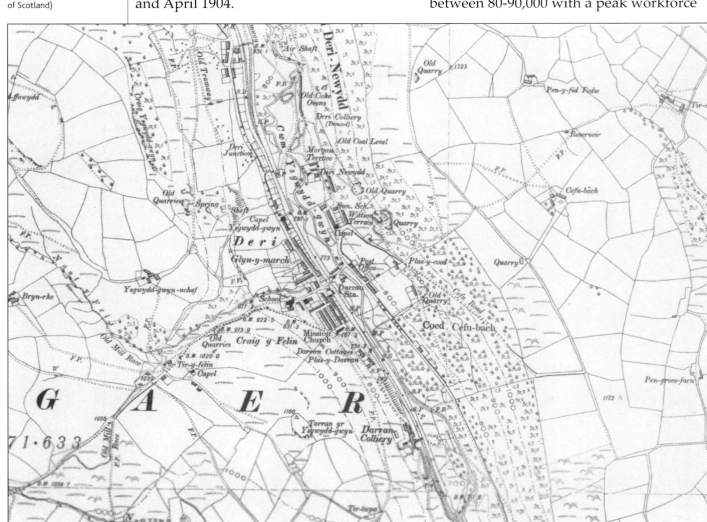

of 272 men. PD acquired almost all the share capital of the Rhymney Iron Co. Ltd. in 1922 and closed the Darran Colliery in 1923 with the siding connection removed in 1927.

Just north of the Darran Colliery was the Deri Newydd pit, opened in 1864 to exploit seams of coal and fireclay, with the first wagons sent to Cardiff Docks in September of that year. The pit had no weighbridge and estimated weights had to be accepted from the colliery. The pit was bought by Benjamin Wood in 1872 but he was bankrupt in 1875 and the pit was put up for auction when the contents were described as of 108 acres, three seams of coal at 60, 95 and 300 yards depth, though only the first was being worked, and 45 coke ovens. There were no bids for the pit and it was again auctioned in April 1877, being declared abandoned by October of that year.

Darran & Deri station as seen in 1905 ... and again in July 1960. (Michael Hale/GWT)

Three views of Darran & Deri platforms in the snow of December 1962, the first looking south, the third looking north.
(All John Hodge)

Darran & Deri station – Rhymney Railway end-on junction with the Brecon & Merthyr.

Darran & Deri Up Platform on 27 September 1958. (R.J. Buckley/Initial Photographics)

The station as on 4 August 1963, closed but still all intact. (Garth Tilt)

Running into Darran & Deri, 3798 heads the 12.10pm Brecon to Newport, the return working of the 8.30am ex-Newport on 27 April 1962. (W.G. Sumner)

The 8.30am Newport to Brecon calls at Darran & Deri behind Ebbw's 3700 on 12 October 1962. (W.G. Sumner)

Looking down on Darran & Deri as a train of coal for treatment at Ogilvie heads for the colliery on 2 April 1964. (Trevor Owen/Colour Rail)

Three views of the 1pm Dowlais Central to Bargoed two coach train arriving at Darran & Deri, at the platform and leaving the station on 27 April 1962.
(All W.G. Sumner)

Latterly there were a few DMU operated services between Bargoed and Fochriw/Dowlais Top, as here with a 3car set on the 1.38pm Bargoed to Fochriw on 27 April 1962. (W.G. Sumner)

The 9.55am Queen Street to Dowlais Top DMU departs Darran & Deri at 11.41 on the last stage of its journey, to return from Dowlais Top at 12.47pm. (Malcolm James)

Ogilvie Village Halt/ Ogilvie Colliery

Near the start of the branch from Deri Jct. into Ogilvie Colliery was the single-platform passenger station of Ogilvie Village Halt 21m. 47ch. from Newport, on a 1 in 35 reverse gradient going north, on the single line from Deri Junction to Fochriw

Between Darran & Deri and Ogilvie Village Halt were a further group of pits and levels known as Cil Haul with sidings on the west side of the running lines. The pits were owned for the whole of their existence from 1864-87 by the Bargoed Coal Co. Ltd. who also owned the nearby Cwmllwydrew colliery to the north. Production of house coal appears to have been intermittent but was constant between 1883-87 with 47,100 tons in 1887 when the pit was abandoned. Also part of the complex was the Cil Haul Level made up of the Bargoed, Cwm and Old Cil levels, all producing house coal from the Brithdir seam. The Bargoed Level, owned by the Bargoed Coal Co. operated in 1875-6, with the Cwm Level also owned by the same company working between 1887-92 when the sidings serving the site were removed. The Old Cil Haul Level came into being in 1922 owned by Hughes & Price and operated between 1922-29, when it was closed. It re-opened in 1931 owned by Rees Price but following poor production figures, the PSA was terminated by the GWR in 1939 and the site shown as abandoned in 1940.

At Deri Junction, just north of Darran & Deri station, a branch went off north to Ogilvie Colliery. This colliery was one of the latest to be developed in the South Wales coalfield and was first to be known as Deri where Guest Keen & Nettlefolds started developments in 1902/3. This proved abortive and in 1915 Powell Duffryn obtained a lease of the site and began sinking a new pit very close to the former Cil Haul Colliery, just under a mile north of Deri Junction. The new Ogilvie Colliery was opened by Powell Duffryn Steam Coal Co. Ltd. in 1923, with access on its own branch line from Deri Jct. which ran parallel to the Rhymney Railway line. There were two pits, North and South and 3-400 miners were employed at the opening, with a colliers' platform provided for rail conveyance from Bargoed. The two pits were opened from 1922 with 877 men employed in 1923. The numbers increased to over 1500 in 1931 but fell during the 1930s recession to around 1,000 and did not rise above that level again until the 1960s.

Always a steam coal pit, Ogilvie worked the Red and Lower Four Feet seams until 1927 and the Rhas Las, Red, Upper Four Feet and Yard Upper Four Feet seams and the Yard from 1937 until

Deri Junction which controlled the entrance into Ogilvie Colliery, seen from a northbound train to Brecon in April 1962.
(R.H. Marrows)

The layout at Deri Jct. as a 2251 Class heads north with a Newport to Brecon service. (T. McCarthy Collection)

Deri Jct. in the process of track recovery on 8 August 1964. (Garth Tilt)

Deri Jct. with only the track into Ogilvie left in situ on 15 October 1967. (Garth Tilt)

Another view of the layout at Deri Junction on 16 April 1963. (Jeff Stone)

Between Deri Junction and Ogilvie Village Halt where the double track changed to single, 5696 heads a Bargoed to Dowlais Top service on 9 May 1959. (R.O. Tuck/ Rail Archive Stephenson)

1968, the last five years of the pit's life spent working on the Lower Four Feet and the Seven Feet seams, several of the others having been worked out.

At Nationalisation in January 1947, details of the colliery were given as North Pit 483 yards (467 to winding level), 20ft diameter coal winding downcast, and South Pit 566 yards (545 to winding level) 20ft diameter coal winding upcast. In March 1953, approval was given for a reconstruction scheme, involving the closure of McLaren and Pidwellt Drift Mine and underground linking and use of Rhymney Merthyr, a closed colliery, for man-riding and ventilation. The overall cost was £5m, with 300 contractors' staff employed on the surface of the mine, modernising facilities. A new pit bottom 50 yards higher was made in the North pit and a new locomotive road was driven northwards to an area of virgin coal which would link into the output from Pidwellt and McLaren. The 1,100hp winding engine in the north pit was retained and double decked, two mine cars per deck, and carriages installed that could handle 336 tons of coal per hour. The coal reserves of McLaren and Rhymney Merthyr collieries were assigned to Ogilvie and the collieries linked underground. The NCB estimated that this would give the colliery a life of 60 years. The last output figures for McLaren gave 143,361tons in 1957. Pidwellt had closed in 1953 and Rhymney Merthyr then employed only seven men underground. The absorption of McLaren was achieved in July 1958.

Before the absorption, Ogilvie's annual output had been: 1954, 247,400 tons; 1955, 266,100; 1956, 303,800; and 1957, 275,500.

Output for 1958, the year of the absorption, was 279,900, but by 1961 this had risen to 352,000 tons and in 1964/5 to 347,000, all classed as semi-bituminous blender. A serious fire broke out in February 1971 resulting in the whole of the south side of the pit being sealed off and the abandonment of the Seven Feet seam reserves, production being concentrated on the Five Feet seam. Four years later the NCB closed the colliery, probably due to the effect of the fire as the reason given was the exhaustion of workable reserves, closure being effected from March 1975.

Full employment figures are available for the entire existence of Ogilvie. They show that in the second year of production, 1924, there were already over 1,000 miners working there, 996 underground and 167 on the surface. This continued to rise and by the end of the 1920s, there were 1,339/202 in 1929, with a peak of 1,356/200 in 1931, after which the depression of the 1930s reduced the number to just over one thousand. The post war years saw the totals at just under 1,000 but from 1956 to 1960 they were given each year as 933/178 and during the 1960s rose again to a peak of 1,328/254

The same train pulling away from Ogilvie Village halt.
(R.O. Tuck)

Two more views of the halt, the first from the 8.3am Newport to Brecon on 12 October 1962, and the second from a Brecon bound train on 2 May 1959. (W.G. Sumner and S. Rickard/ D.K. Jones J&J Collection)

Though the track has been lifted through Ogilvie Village Halt, Ogilvie Colliery is still active with the line from Deri Jct. seen on the right as on 15 October 1967. (Garth Tilt)

Two views of Ogilvie Colliery Platform with 9638 on the 12.50pm Dowlais Central to Bargoed Workmen's train on 27 April 1962. (Both W.G. Sumner)

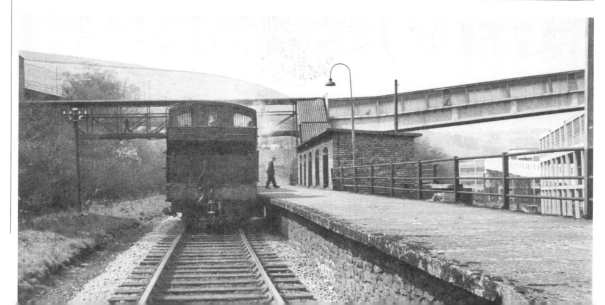

Three views of Ogilvie Colliery Platform and Ogilvie Colliery with snow on the ground in December 1962. (All John Hodge)

Ogilvie Colliery.
(R. Lawrence Collection)

A train from Mclaren of reclaimed tip coal reaches the end of its journey at Ogilvie Colliery where the coal will be washed and blended for supply to Port Talbot Steelworks on 3 April 1965. The load even for an assisted 56XX was in practice only fifteen wagons as seen here due to the gradient of 1 in 43 between Bargoed and Ogilvie. (T.B. Owen/ Colour Rail)

Just north of Ogilvie, New Brithdir Nos. 1-4 are originally shown, but these were probably small levels. Much use was made of the name Brithdir, from coal seams being extended into colliery names and it has not been possible to pinpoint the exact details of these pits or levels. Neither has it been possible to find details of the Plantation and Old Plantation levels located just north of New Brithdir, though a Plantation is shown as being explored and then abandoned in 1948. These were located in the Fochriw area at the very northern edge of the coalfield where it is likely that seams were easily accessed in the mid-nineteenth century, exhausted and quickly abandoned.

Fochriw

Fochriw station, at 23m.68ch. from Newport, had staggered platforms creating a long passenger station working area on a 1 in 300 reverse gradient going north. There was no footbridge between platforms and passengers had to use a boarded crossing located at the south end of the down platform and north end of the Up. For passengers detraining from Down trains and leaving the station, this entailed crossing right in front of the train which had just arrived.

Fochriw Junction, at 24m.33ch. from Newport, was linked to Fochriw Colliery, the Pantywaun Mineral Railway and to Cwmbargoed on the Taff Bargoed line from Ystrad Mynach South to Dowlais Caeharris. For many years, Fochriw Jct. had its own signal box, which was replaced by a Ground Frame in 1925. From that date, its continued usefulness is not clear, Fochriw Colliery and the pits along the Pantywaun Railway having closed. Nevertheless, the connection appears to have survived until the 1950s, purely as a link between the two lines.

Fochriw Colliery was one of the most northerly collieries in this part of the coalfield, and the last colliery to be served by the Brecon-bound B&M line. This steam coal colliery consisted of two

pits both operating between 1886 and 1924. No. 1 Pit worked the Upper Four Feet and Big seams, plus the Two Feet Nine between 1908-15, while No. 2 Pit worked the Rhas Las and Red seams. With its proximity to Dowlais, it is not surprising that Fochriw (or Vochryw / Vochriew) Colliery was opened by the Dowlais Iron Co., at the height of their iron making prowess in the mid-nineteenth century, actually commencing sinking in 1856. No. 1 Pit reached full production by June 1863 and No. 2 by September 1866. Running powers for the LNWR from Dowlais Top were agreed from 1872 with a turnout also facing north as well as south at the colliery junction. In 1891 the Downcast depth of No. 1 (Bedlinog) Pit was given as 433ft and the No. 2 (Fochriw) Upcast as 375ft with a maximum production in 1894 of 412,700 tons. In 1898 there was a five month long strike at the colliery during which there were heavy falls of rock and water and on the introduction of a washery in 1898, there were further disputes regarding the declaration of payment tonnages. In 1901 the colliery passed to the ownership of Guest Keen & Co. Ltd. who announced that the two year dispute had been settled. In 1902, ownership was vested in Guest, Keen & Nettlefolds Ltd. In 1910, Fochriw No. 1 Pit was producing 1,900 tons per week from the Upper Two Feet Nine and Upper Four Feet seams with plans to open the Six Feet seam. No. 2 Pit was producing 3,900 tons per week from the Big, Red and Rhas Las seams. There were however geological problems at the colliery with a serious roof fall in mid-1916 and in 1921 problems occurred with the shafts, with water incursion still a problem. The colliery was closed on 30 April 1924 and the plant and materials put up for auction in October 1925.

At the turn of the twentieth century, there were some 1,440 miners employed at Fochriw which increased to over 2,000 in 1914/5, with still 1,878 at closure in 1924.

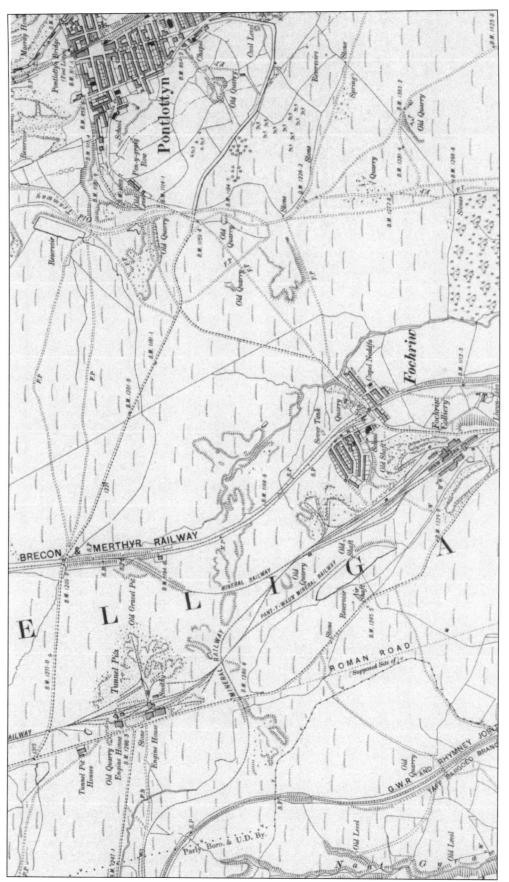

OS Map of the Fochriw area at the turn of the twentieth century, showing the colliery and the various mineral lines in use between the area and Dowlais Ironworks and connecting into the B&M line. Tunnel Pits was an important colliery on this network, which stretched to Pantywaun. (National Library of Scotland)

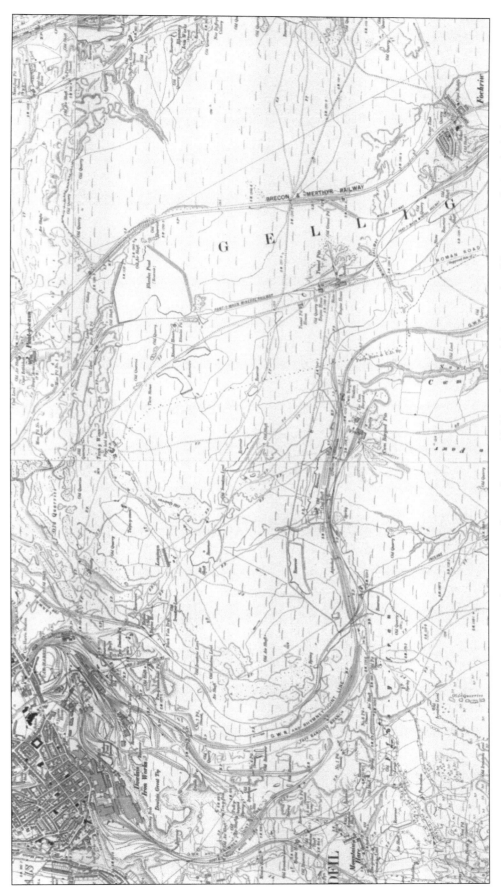

OS Map of the area between Fochriw and Pantywaun. This was part of a very large coalfield serving Dowlais Ironworks with many small pits which closed when the Ironworks closed. Note the relatively straight trajectory of the B&M line in comparison with the later GWR & RR Joint line from Ystrad Mynach to Dowlais Cae Harris on the centre/left of the map. (National Library of Scotland)

Fochriw Station
with its staggered
platforms, looking
north in June 1962.
(Michael Hale/GWT)

Fochriw down
platform seen from
the north end of
the up platform on
3 September 1962.
(Michael Roach)

Fochriw Up Platform
looking south from
the south end of the
Down Platform on
3 September 1962.
(Michael Roach)

Another view of Fochriw looking north to the down platform where a 56XX heads a Dowlais Central to Bargoed two coach service target RC. (SLS)

A 1910 view of Fochriw Up Platform from the south end of the Down Platform. (Lens of Sutton)

A close-up view of the Up Platform from the 11.38am DMU from Bargoed to Dowlais Top in December 1962. (John Hodge)

Fochriw SB and Down platform in December 1962. The signal box was by McKenzie & Holland, housing a 12-lever frame, and closed in August 1963.
(John Hodge)

A look along the northbound platform as the 11.15am Newport to Brecon is accommodated on 13 July 1962.
(Robert Darlaston)

The driver of 3706 on a Newport to Brecon service takes the token through to Dowlais Top in this 1960 view.
(Monmouthshire Railway Society)

3201 leaves Fochriw with the 11.15am Newport to Brecon on 3 September 1962. (Michael Roach)

2227 heads the daily Bassaleg to Brecon freight passing Fochriw on 14 August 1957, much of the load consisting of domestic coal for local coal merchants en route. (R.O. Tuck)

Another view of the daily Bassaleg to Brecon freight as it passes Fochriw, taken from the upside on 14 August 1957. (S. Rickard/ D.K. Jones J&J Collection)

9638 at the Down Platform with the 1.10pm Pant to Bargoed service on 27 April 1962. By this time, the local goods siding had been lifted and the protecting signal arm removed. (W.G. Sumner)

Pontypool Road's 6652 with the return empty Dowlais ICI ammonia tanks passing Fochriw on 3 September 1962. (Michael Roach)

2298 has arrived at Fochriw with the 2.5pm Brecon to Newport and passengers are leaving the platform via the boarded crossing between the platforms on 29 September 1962. (W.G. Sumner)

A 56XX stops at the signal box to hand over the token from Dowlais Top with a short down freight on 28 April 1962. (Alan Jarvis/SLS)

Two views of new Ebbw Junction acquisition 2247 first running into Fochriw with the 2.15pm Brecon to Newport and then departing on 28 April 1962. (Alan Jarvis/SLS)

The Brecon to Bassaleg freight passing through Fochriw and composed of a complete train of empty mineral wagons off up loaded domestic coal on 14 August 1957 (S. Rickard / D.K. Jones J&J Collection)

4611 starts away south from Fochriw with a Brecon to Newport train as a group of ladies leaves the train and station via the Up Platform on 22 December 1962, with only a week to go before withdrawal of the passenger service and closure of the line. (M.B. Warburton)

The 12.47pm Dowlais Top to Cardiff Queen Street DMU pauses at the SB to exchange tokens on 28 April 1962. (Alan Jarvis/SLS)

7736 with the 8.30am Newport to Brecon calls at Fochriw on 1 August 1959, one of the last recordings of an older type pannier, soon to be replaced by the 8750 class.
(T.B. Owen/Colour Rail)

The token is exchanged by the Fochriw signalman for the one to Dowlais Top with the driver of the 11.15am Newport to Brecon at 12.35pm on 18 July 1959.
(R.E. Toop)

The site of the former Fochriw station as at 15 October 1967.
(Garth Tilt)

The former B&M line down the Darran Valley through Fochriw looking towards Ogilvie and Darran & Deri down the steep incline. (Ken Mumford Presentations)

Two views of the windswept Fochriw Colliery Junction with its attendant coal tips but no traffic as on 8 August 1964. (Garth Tilt)

Two colliery shunters, the first under repair at Fochriw Colliery on 14 August 1948.
(A.C. Sterndale)

Colliery shunter No. 29 at Fochriw Colliery on 14 August 1948.
(A.C. Sterndale)

A lovely snowy landscape on the last day of operation as 4627 heads north with the 11.15am Newport to Brecon.
(R.O. Tuck)

North of Fochriw, 7736 makes a fine shot of the mountainous landscape with the 11.15am Newport to Brecon on 9 May 1959… and heads away north. (Both R.O. Tuck)

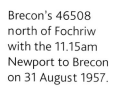

Brecon's 46508 north of Fochriw with the 11.15am Newport to Brecon on 31 August 1957.

Pantywaun Halt

Pantywaun (Pantywaen) Halt at 25m. 53ch. from Newport stood on a falling gradient of 1 in 59 going north and was a late addition to the line. It was only opened during the war on 22 December 1941 to facilitate miners' travel to the local opencast site and also to the pits to the south at Ogilvie and Groesfaen, and lasted until the final closure of the line in December 1962. The village of Pantywaun was small with only fifty or so houses, though with the usual disproportionate three pubs and three churches. Under the extension of the Cwmbargoed Royal Arms Opencast site by Taylor Woodrow from the late 1960s, the village completely disappeared. One of the public houses was the Royal Arms and this name was taken for the opencast site. Though the halt had no facilities on the single platform, there was a ticket office and small waiting room on a nearby bridge, the weather at this point being very inclement on many occasions.

The village of Pantywaun originally lay in the centre of a very heavy mining area with five pits all supplying the Dowlais Iron Works. The cessation of steel making at Dowlais in 1935 with the opening of the East Moors plant at Cardiff Docks, had a huge effect on all the mines in the area used to supply the works and killed them overnight. The five pits in the immediate area around Pantywaun were the Carnau Drift on the north side of the B&M line and four pits on the south side of the line, from south to north the Four Feet Pit, Mine Pit No. 1, Mine Pit No. 2 and Pantywaun Pit.

The Carnau (or Carno) Mine in its heyday was a large complex with about twenty sidings feeding off the loading point. It was operative during the nineteenth century and was shown as abandoned pre-1872. An attempt was made to start it up again in 1947 by I. Smith but in 1951 it was again shown as abandoned.

The most prolific section of the Pantywaun pits was the Lower Four feet, which was the closest section to Fochriw, located on the private Pantywaun Railway between Fochriw and Dowlais Iron Works. Though the pit was operative pre-1850, in 1851 it was shown as owned by Sir John Josiah Guest and Edward John Hutchins trading as the Dowlais Iron Co., Guest, Lewis & Co., and as Guest & Co. Figures for its operation are available from 1871 to 1887 when it ceased production. By 1877, it was producing around 40,000 tons a year, but this reduced during the 1880s to under 20,000 and it was closed in 1887.

The Pant y Waun pit itself lay south of the Carnau Drift with the line running between the two, crossing over the B&M

The expansive view north of Fochriw with grassed over coal tips from the former colliery there, as 5635 works a two coach Bargoed to Pant service on 1 August 1959.
(T.B. Owen/Colour Rail)

line well north of where the Halt would be developed in years to come. East of Pantywaun Pit was Mine Pit No. 2 and then Mine Pit No. 1, lying between the main pit and the Lower Four Feet Pit as dealt with above. These areas of mine pits and patches had been worked for many years during the early and mid-nineteenth century to supply the Dowlais Iron Works and in April 1851 *The Welshman* reported that 'A rich vein of coal was struck at Pantywaun new pit last week. On 29th March the engine and wagons brought down many tons to the works.' The boiler there blew up in 1869 but in March 1874 the coal from the pit was declared of inferior quality and the Works stated it would not accept any further coal from that pit. For its last two years of production, all coal from Pantywaun pit was despatched through Fochriw Colliery. In 1912 the pit was listed as abandoned. Efforts were made in future years to work the site but were terminated in 1948. Figures for the period 1871-75 show a normal annual level of production of 3-4,000 tons, but after the ultimatum from the Dowlais Iron Works, this rose to 4,800 in 1876 and 8,600 in 1877.

Though each of these pits was on private land, there was a link line from each to the Four Feet Pit, from where there was a long connecting line into the B&M single line (known as No. 2 Siding), alongside which a relief siding was provided to hold empty wagons and loaded awaiting collection. There was a signal box at the junction with the B&M line, a new frame for which was installed in October 1893. All connections and sidings were removed in June 1939.

With the high level of movement at Pantywaen, the B&M used the layout as a marshalling point for all freight traffic in the area. Trains were terminated and started at Pantywaen from and to the southern and northern sections of the B&M until coal production in the area ceased in 1936 when its role as a freight staging point ceased, giving rise to the creation of the through working between Bassaleg and Brecon and return.

With the cessation of operations at each of the Pantywaun sites and the closure of the steel making process at Dowlais Works in 1936, the miners from the Pantywaun area were forced to travel to Ogilvie, Groesfaen and Bargoed Pits for employment and their travel problems led the B&M to open the Pantywaun Halt at 24m.69ch. on 22 December 1941 so that they could use the Dowlais Central to Bargoed Miners services from their own station instead of having to use the Dowlais Top station.

Much of the area north and east of Fochriw, including the former Pantywaun coalfield, is now included in the Ffos y Fran Opencast site, a huge area stretching north from east of Merthyr to include the former coal producing area of Pantywaun which supplied the Dowlais Ironworks, much consisting of shallow mines, pits, levels and drifts at the very north end of the South Wales coalfield, where coal seams were close to the surface. On the former B&M line, the area north of Fochriw where the colliery closed in the late 1950s and the area north to Pantywaun and almost to Dowlais Top, is included, though much of this was included in the Cwmbargoed Opencast area previously. The reclaimed coal was formerly used at Aberthaw Power Station, but this flow ceased from March 2020 when the station stopped burning fossil fuel, and a higher volatile coal is now produced suitable for use in the production of steel, which is conveyed to Port Talbot Steelworks. A third flow is current, that to Hope Valley Cement Works on the Manchester-Sheffield line. The reclaimed coal is conveyed by high-capacity vehicles to Cwmbargoed Washery where it is washed and graded for onward conveyance. Up to 150,000 tons a year is produced from the Cwmbargoed plant.

Opencast mining on such a large scale has produced several social problems which have had to be addressed, such

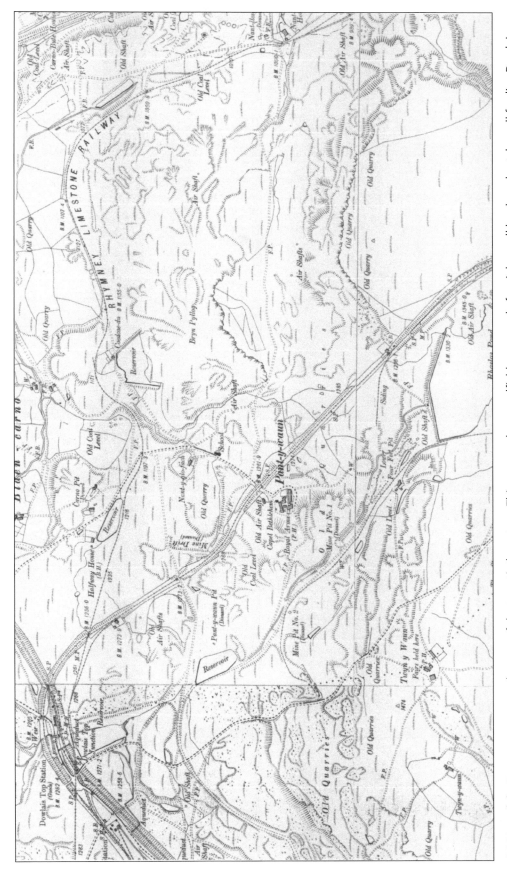

OS Map of the Pantywaun area at the turn of the twentieth century. This was one huge coalfield composed of mainly small levels and patches, all feeding Dowlais Ironworks. All these closed with the closure of Dowlais Ironworks, but were then embraced into the Cwmbargoed Opencast centre and are now included in the Ffos y Fran development in which coal from tips and other deposits is brought by road into Cwmbargoed where it is washed and blended to go forward in modern 100ton wagons, first to Aberthaw Power Station, but now to Port Talbot Steelworks and Hope cement Works, following the closure of Aberthaw as a coal burning station.
(National Library of Scotland)

The short Pantywaun
Halt in the snow
in December 1962.
(John Hodge)

5615 with the
11.35am SO Bargoed
to Dowlais Top runs
into Pantywaun Halt
on 24 May 1958.
(Michael Hale/GWT)

9638 heading south
with the 1.10pm
Pant to Bargoed
on 27 April 1962.
(W.G. Sumner)

A pannier hauled Bargoed to Dowlais Top near Pantywaun, on this windswept former coalfield, dotted with coal tips from former activity.
(Ken Mumford Presentations)

as dust carried by the winds from the high ground to residential areas in Merthyr producing poor air quality, noise from blasting, and flooding and other water problems from the blocking of underground water channels, inter alia. However, coal is required in the production of steel and the flow from Cwmbargoed reduces the amount to be imported. Cwmbargoed will be included in a future book on the upper Rhymney Valley.

Dowlais Top

Dowlais Top at 26m.49ch. from Newport and standing on more-or-less flat ground at 1 in 300 facing north, was one of four stations at the once great town of Dowlais when it ranked alongside Merthyr as the most important towns in the country due to its production of iron, at that time used in the production of everything from rails to cannon balls. Two of these stations belonged to the B&M, Dowlais Central (the previous Lloyd Street) being the original terminus of the line, before its development south from Pant to Bargoed. Dowlais High Street was on the Merthyr, Tredegar and Abergavenny line and Dowlais Caeharris was a Dowlais Rhymney terminus on the line from Ystrad Mynach. Dowlais Top was located just north of Dowlais Junction, the connection off the MT&A into the B&M which closed in 1935. Both this and Dowlais Top station were located on the Dowlais Moors to the north of the town of Dowlais, and were renowned for their windswept nature, with many helpings of snow in the average winter.

At the south end of the Up and Down platform station was the signal box on the downside with a gate operated level crossing carrying the road that ran through the village. The station remained in much the same state throughout its life, with main facilities on the Up side and just a shelter, often very necessary, on the Down. A bus service operated from the station to and from Merthyr.

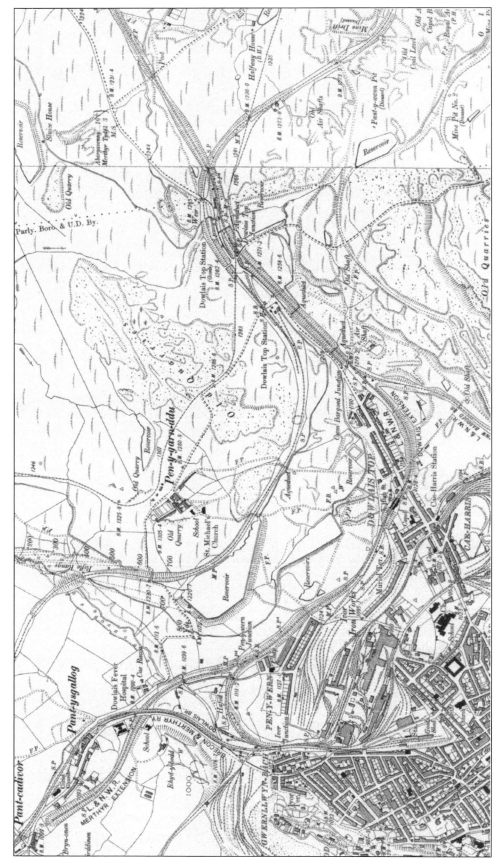

An OS Map of Dowlais Top and Pantyscallog for 1888-1913 showing the B&M and LNWR lines in that area. (National Library of Scotland)

Dowlais Top in the snow – a regular scene in winter. This view in December 1962. (John Hodge)

A close-up of the signal box and level crossing on 3 September 1962. The signal box was a brick-built McKenzie & Holland structure, housing a 19-lever frame. (Michael Roach)

A distant view of the station area on 23 August 1961. (Edwin Wilmshirst)

The Up Platform in the snow as the photographer has just detrained from the 11.35am DMU from Bargoed.
(John Hodge)

The final day of operation on 29 December 1962 saw snow on the ground, though only a covering. Here 4679 has charge of the 12.10pm Brecon to Newport while a three car DMU works the 11.38am from Bargoed which will later return with the 12.47pm to Cardiff Queen Street.
(R.O. Tuck)

Only a week earlier the sun shone brightly as the 11.15am from Newport ran in over the level crossing with 4679 again in charge.
(Gerald T. Robinson)

A summer scene as the staff await the arrival of the next service to Brecon which is hauled by a 2251 Class engine. (SLS)

During the period when Standard Class 2MTs worked the line from Brecon shed, 46508 with the 11.15am from Newport stands next to the 12.47pm to Queen Street DMU on 3 October 1959. (F.K. Davies)

4679 runs into Dowlais Top on the last day of operation with the 12.10pm from Brecon. (R.O. Tuck)

Looking north from Dowlais Top, the 11.15am Newport to Brecon departs on the last day of service on 29 December 1962, as photographer Bob Tuck looks on. (John Hodge)

2298 starts away from the station with the 2.5pm from Brecon on 12 October 1962. (W.G. Sumner)

The Dowlais Top signalman fights to stand upright on the south end of the up platform against the blustering wind across the Dowlais Moors as Oswestry's 2240 runs in with the 11.15am Newport to Brecon, the return working of the 7.35am from Brecon in 1959. At this time, it was common for Oswestry to provide a 2251 Class for the Brecon turns to Newport. The 12.47pm DMU service to Cardiff Queen Street stands at the down platform. (Ken Mumford Presentations)

Ex-Rhymney AP 78 on a Bargoed to Dowlais Central service calling at Dowlais Top. (Allan Pym Collection)

Former TVR 04 333 runs into Dowlais Top with the 1.14pm Dowlais Central to Bargoed Workmen's service, composed of all clerestory-roofed stock on 26 April 1948. (W.A. Camwell/SLS)

Pannier 3700 has charge of the 8.3am from Newport as it pulls away from the station on 12 October 1962. (W.G. Sumner)

3747 runs in with the 8.30am from Newport on 29 September 1962 and will return from Brecon with the 12.10pm down. (David Lawrence/Hugh Davies Collection)

3691 prepares to start away northwards with the 11.15am from Newport on 27 April 1962. (W.G. Sumner)

In addition to the Brecon services, Dowlais Top was also served by the Dowlais Central-Pant-Bargoed services. Here 9638 of Merthyr depot runs in with the 12.58pm Dowlais Central to Bargoed train on 27 April 1962. (W.G. Sumner)

In earlier times, the Dean Goods 2301 Class 0-6-0s were a common sight on the line as here with 2407 working the empty ICI Ammonia tanks back to Dowlais Central on 26 April 1948. (SLS)

A further variation in power as the return empty tankers are worked through on the last day of operation by Pontypool Road's 6693. (R.O. Tuck)

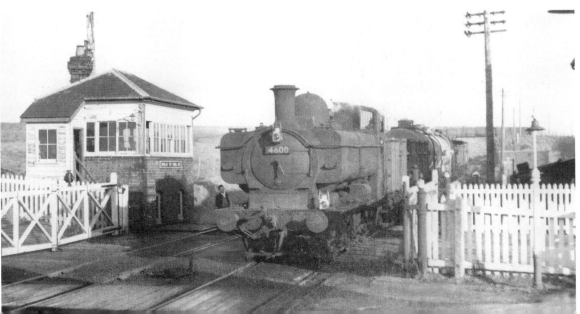

Over fourteen years later and the same train is in the hands of Pontypool Road Pannier 4600 as it crosses the level crossing at the south end of the station on 22 December 1962. Note the use of barrier wagons in later years.
(Gerald T. Robinson)

The loaded ammonia tanks have come down from Pant, where they have reversed from the line from Dowlais Central and here the train worked by Pontypool Road's 6652 is banked by 9618. At Dowlais Top 9618 runs round the train and pilots 6652 southwards.
(Both Michael Roach)

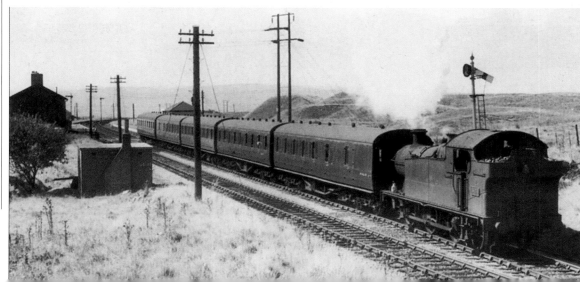

The 12.47SO Dowlais Top to Cardiff Queen Street pulls away from the starting point with a 56XX in charge.
(Ken Mumford Presentations)

The Brecon to Bassaleg Goods rejoins the single line south of Dowlais Top with its usual load of empty minerals, today quite lengthy, with engine 2287 on 7 July 1950. (T.C. Cole)

Leaving Dowlais Top and rejoining the single line, 3634 enjoys the downhill ride with a Brecon to Newport service on 14 August 1957. (D.K. Jones Collection)

A Pant to Bargoed ECS train with 5635 leaves Dowlais Top and crosses the former LNW line on 1 August 1959. (T.B. Owen/Colour Rail)

Another view of Dowlais Top station taken from the Up platform on 22 December 1962, which was a bright sunny day unlike the closure day a week later. (Mark Warburton)

Approaching Dowlais Top from the south on 13 October 1962 on a Newport to Brecon service with a 2251 0-6-0 in charge. (Alan Jarvis)

Departing southwards from Dowlais Top over the level crossing with 8766 on the 12.10pm service from Brecon on 18 May 1959. (Alan Jarvis)

Above: 3634 with a two coach train approaching Dowlais Top with the disused line from Dowlais Central in the centre, as seen on 14 August 1957.

Left: On the sweeping curve approaching Dowlais Top Brecon's 2280 crosses the bridge over the disused line from Dowlais Central with the 11.15am from Newport on 16 May 1959. (D.K. Jones Collection)

Below: Approaching Dowlais Top from Fochriw, there was a connection from the LNWR Abergavenny to Merthyr line. In this 1922 view, wagons of large coal from Bargoed Colliery can be seen on the track presumably to be handed over to the B&M for onward conveyance. The line was closed and lifted in 1935. The bleakness of the Dowlais Moors beyond can be appreciated even though the weather is good in this photograph. (D.K. Jones Collection)

Another view of the 12.47pm to Queen Street, now worked by a DMU, with the recovered former LNW line from Dowlais Central in the foreground.
(Ken Mumford Presentations)

Dowlais Top SB on 10 July 1958.
(H.C. Casserley)

Dowlais Top with tracks removed as on 15 October 1967.
(Garth Tilt)

Pant

Pant station was at 27½ miles from Newport and was located on a relatively flat section of the B&M line from Dowlais Top to approaching Pontsticill. The layout at Pant at 1 in 231 facing north, was unusual in that it was the meeting point of two direct lines, the original line from Brecon to Dowlais and the slightly later line from Brecon to Bargoed/Newport. As such, there was no direct line from Dowlais to Bargoed, other than by reversing north of Pant station at Pant Junction. This was probably due to the rock structure north of the station which prevented the building of a station at that point, the main station on the Brecon/Pontsticill Jct./Bargoed section being to the south, on a fairly tight curve. The platform structure at Pant was triangular with the Up platform to Pontsticill and Brecon and the Down platform to Bargoed on the main route, with a single line platform for Up and Down trains from/to Dowlais Lloyd Street, which became Dowlais Central after the Grouping. The signal box controlling Pant and the junction north of the station was located on the north end of the main platform. A water column was also located near the box which was famous for having a brazier beneath it kept permanently burning in the winter to avoid the water column freezing, it being imperative that engines of northbound trains could take water at this point.

Pant (Glam) station seen from the south end, the station buildings concentrated on the up platform, with not even a shelter on the down.
(Lens of Sutton)

Pant from the south end with tracks no longer in use on 4 August 1963.
(Garth Tilt)

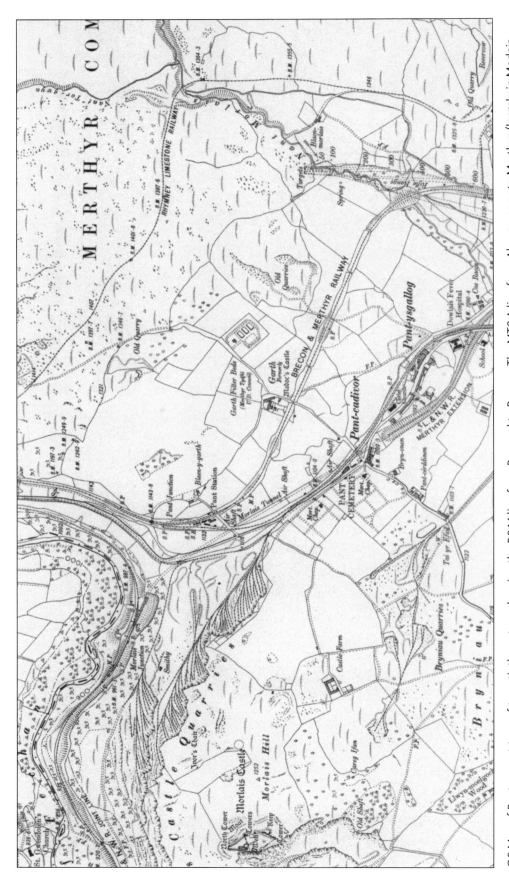

OS Map of Pant area at turn of twentieth century showing the B&M line from Bargoed to Brecon, The MT&A line from Abergavenny to Merthyr (largely in Morlais Tunnel at this point) and the Rhymney Limestone Railway. (National Library of Scotland)

Pant Down Platform in the snow looking south in December 1962. (John Hodge)

Pant platform on the Dowlais branch line with Pant SB at the north end of the Bargoed line platform. (Lens of Sutton)

An early posed shot at Pant with a B&M 0-6-0T on an Up freight service. (Great Western Trust)

One of the two 0-6-0STs that worked the Merthyr to Pontsticill and Dowlais services in pre-Grouping days, 17, at Pant c1922.
(LCGB Collection/NRM)

Another shot of 17 working back from Dowlais Central to Pant and seen at the small side platform at Pant on the Dowlais line, c1922.
(LCGB Collection/NRM)

Taking water at the north end of Pant station, 17 prepares to work back to Pontsticill on turn D1 c1922. The high standard of cleaning is evident in these early views.
(LCGB Collection/NRM)

With the connecting train from Dowlais in the background, one of the newer 0-6-2Ts built to Rhymney Railway design in 1915 leaves Pant with the 2.17pm to Brecon c1922. These engines ended their days numbered 421-436, allocated to depots along the main line e.g. Newport Ebbw and Pill, Cardiff Canton and Radyr after ending their pre-Grouping days at Bassaleg and Brecon. (LCGB Collection/NRM)

Pant station in 1922 with the then customary milk churns on a platform barrow. (D.K. Jones Collection)

9638 Has just run round the 12.58pm from Dowlais Central and brings the train into Pant for its journey on to Bargoed on 27 April 1962. (W.G. Sumner)

A Bargoed to Dowlais Central train runs into Pant on 3 September 1962 with a Merthyr pannier running bunker-first.
(Michael Roach)

2298 brings the 2.5pm Brecon to Newport round the curve into Pant, seen at the north end of the station, on 3 September 1962.
(Michael Roach)

Waiting departure, 2298 stands at Pant with the 2.5pm Brecon to Newport in September 1962.
(Paul Riley Restoration & Archiving Trust)

Pant Down Platform; 9638 awaits departure with the 12.58pm Dowlais Central to Bargoed on 27 April 1962. The waiting shelter on the down platform seen here was a later provision. (W.G. Sumner)

Ebbw's 7774 at Pant with a Brecon to Newport service on 3 October 1959. For the final years of the service, the older flat-roofed panniers of the 57XX, 77XX and early 87XX series were replaced by the newer rounded-roofed 36XX, 37XX, 46XX, later 87XX, 96XX and 97XX. (F.K. Davies)

Facing south at Pant, 9644 has the road with a Brecon to Newport service on 4 November 1961. It was the practice to run engine-first in both directions on Brecon services from/to Newport, engines being turned using the turntables at both Brecon and Newport stations. (W.G. Sumner)

3700 takes a well-earned drink at the Pant water column working the 8.30am Newport to Brecon on 12 October 1962. (Both W.G. Sumner)

4635 comes EBV off the Dowlais Central branch on 11 April 1962. (Jeff Stone)

In snowy conditions on the last day of service, as the 8.30am from Newport approaches Pant … and stands at the up platform awaiting departure on 27 December 1962. (Both Jeff Stone)

Another view of the north end of the station, this time in April snow, on 27 April 1962. (Malcolm James)

Above: Approaching Pant from Dowlais Top with 3638 on the 11.15am Newport to Brecon on 2 May 1959. (S. Rickard/D.K. Jones J&J Collection)

Below left: Pant signal box at the north end of the Up Platform. This was a McKenzie & Holland design, later modified to accommodate a stove in lieu of a fireplace, and sporting two GWR cast nameboards. (R.H. Marrows)

Below right: Pant Signal Box at the north end of the Up Platform with the water column as seen on 27th January 1962. The water column was kept heated whenever there was a risk of very cold weather. (P.J. Garland/ Roger Carpenter Colln.)

Two views of the empty Dowlais ammonia tanks at Pant Jct. where the Dowlais branch leaves the line to Bargoed and Newport. The first shot shows Pontypool Road's 6652 passing the bracket signal for the branch… and the second shows the train taking the single line to Dowlais, both views on 3 September 1962. (Michael Roach)

Pant with two of the three platforms occupied in the 1950s. (SLS)

Recently ex-Caerphilly Works, Ebbw Jct. Pannier 8766 with the 8.30am Newport to Brecon on 18 May 1959. (Alan Jarvis/SLS)

Waiting at Pant station on the Dowlais line, 9675 with the U2 service to Dowlais Central. 9675 would have been allocated to Dowlais sub shed at this time. (Ken Mumford Presentations)

The layout north of Pant on 4 August 1963 with the line to Dowlais still in daily use by the ammonia traffic. (Garth Tilt)

Two views of Pant with 9744 on the 11.15am Newport to Brecon on 19 June 1962. (Garth Tilt)

Pant is now completely bereft of any tracks on 15 October 1967. (Garth Tilt)

Pontsticill Junction

Between Pant and Pontsticill Junction, the main B&M line ran parallel with the Merthyr to Pontsticill Jct. branch, this rising gradually to the level of the main line as it approached the junction. This was also the beginning of the very scenic nature of the line as it now ran alongside the reservoirs at the south end of the Brecon Beacons, making it one of the most attractive stretches of line in the country. Pontsticill Junction station lay at 29m.63ch. from Newport at 1 in 198 facing north and was the main station on the line between Bargoed and Talyllyn Jct., the meeting point for trains on the main Newport to Brecon route and those coming in from Merthyr. Dating from the early years of the B&M when much freight and passenger traffic was exchanged between the two lines at this station, there were

Map of the Pontsticill area at the turn of the 20th Century. (National Library of Scotland)

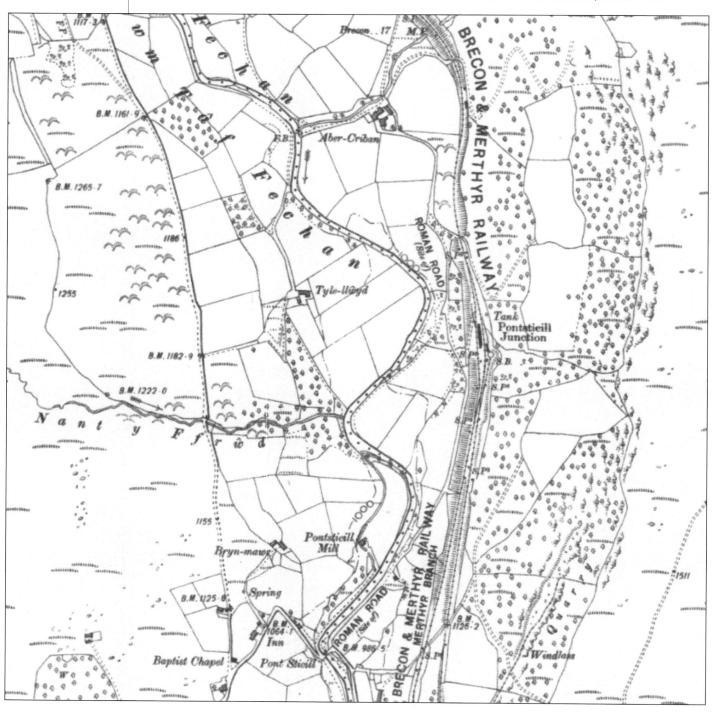

The view approaching Pontsticill from Pant showing Taf Fechan Reservoir and the Merthyr branch line on 2 May 1959. (S. Rickard/D.K. Jones J&J Collection)

A fine shot of Pontsticill Junction station in the sun on 13 October 1962. The normal practice was for the island platform to be used for the Merthyr service with the Brecon services using the up and down main platforms. The GWR rebuilt the SB top and installed a 52-lever frame in 1930. (W.G. Sumner)

several sidings both on the Up and Down side, including a turntable for use when tender engines were involved, largely off the Mid Wales line, or when tank engines required to be turned in connection with the Seven Mile Bank. Through freight trains from Merthyr to Brecon and reverse and the later Bassaleg to Brecon service were always booked to work at Pontsticill to exchange traffic between the two lines, while the later Dowlais Central ammonia tank trains were often recessed there to allow a passenger train to pass. The signal box controlling all movements at this location, which was renewed in 1885, was located at the south end of the Down platform, on which the main facilities were located, including the station master's house. The Up platform was an island, the west face of which was used by the terminating passenger services from Merthyr, the east face being used by the through Up Brecon services and northbound freights.

In the early years of the twentieth century, and probably before, there were quarries in the high ground on the east side of the line, with tramroads running down to loading points alongside the main line. The

Pontsticill in about 1905 with a saddle tank on a goods service standing in one of the sidings alongside the Merthyr platform. Note the bridge spanning the platforms which was one of only two such structures on the B&M, the other being at Machen, both soon dismantled and not replaced, passengers having to use the boarded crossing at the south end of the platforms to cross the line. (SLS)

Abercriban Quarry had two loading points, one just north of the station with a PSA with the B&M in the name of M. Richards from 1901 to 1934. The other, further north, had a PSA for A.W. Lewis trading as the Abercriban Quarry Co. from 1913-17. Robert McAlpine is also recorded as having a PSA between 1915 and 1926, but whether this referred to the above sidings is unclear.

Further south, on the east side of the line to Pant, was the Baltic Quarry, again with a tramroad bringing stone down to a loading point on the main line, with a PSA to the New Tylerbont Stone & Asphalt Co. Ltd. between 1925 and 1944, though

probably existing before the turn of the century. A serious landslip occurred near this loading point in November 1931.

On the single line to Merthyr which fell away to a lower level on the west side of the main line, there was a loop located opposite the loading point on the main line, but this was declared surplus to requirements and was removed in July 1925, having previously been used to hold freight trains awaiting acceptance into Pontsticill.

Further south towards Pant, was another quarry Tylahaidd, dating from around 1875 which was closed and re-instated by June 1896, but no further details are available.

2218 approaches Pontsticill with the 3pm Newport to Brecon on 1 September 1949. The veteran passenger brakevan on the front of the train is the Thursday Only Swindon Stores Van bound for Brecon. (B.W.L. Brooksbank/Initial Photographics)

CHAPTER 3

PANT TO DOWLAIS CENTRAL

Pant

The Dowlais branch was opened on 19 March 1863, trains from Dowlais initially running non-stop to Pant, to a single line platform on the branch. This was some 15ch. south of the junction with what became the main Bargoed to Brecon line. A contemporary plan shows a single platform on the branch with a run-round loop, a goods shed on a further loop siding, with a turntable off the run-round loop. There was also a connection to the Dowlais Limestone private railway here. In later years, the branch platform at Pant was on a single line with run-round facilities at Pant Jct. just north of the station.

Pantyscallog

This was the only intermediate station on the branch and was opened on 1 October 1910. A single goods siding was provided but lifted some years before the station closed. It was downgraded to a halt in 1945 and was renamed High Level to distinguish from the LNWR station there in 1950, closure coming on 2 May 1960. The OS Map of Dowlais Top also shows Pantysgallog.

The only station between Dowlais Central and Pant was Pantyscallog, here seen from the returning special on 2 May 1964.
(P.J. Garland/Roger Carpenter)

More views of the single line platform at Pantyscallog on 13 October 1962 and on 28 December 1963. The wide formation here is due to a lifted private railway which ran alongside the Dowlais branch, presumably between Dowlais ironworks and limestone quarries. (Jeff Stone, Mike Roach, W.G. Sumner)

Pantyscallog (B&M) on 10 July 1958. (D.K. Jones Collection)

Two train views at Pantyscallog; the first the daily service train from Pant to Dowlais with 4632 in April 1960. (E.T. Gill/ R.K. Blencowe Collection)

The second, the 2 May 1964 SLS special approaching the station en route from Dowlais to Pontsticill. (Jeff Stone)

Pantyscallog after recovery of all tracks as seen on 15 October 1967. (Garth Tilt)

Dowlais (Lloyd Street) / Dowlais Central

This B&M station at the then thriving ironworks town of Dowlais opened to passengers with much ceremony on 23 June 1869. With the Grouping it was renamed by the GWR to Dowlais Central in 1924, one of many stations subject to such renaming. Approaching from Pant, the Dowlais Iron Co. private line serving limestone quarries ran alongside the main line, crossing it, together with a further private line, as Dowlais No. 1 Junction was approached. Here the lofty No. 1 signal box controlled the crossings and the junction with the LNWR line trailing in from Penywern Jct. The ironworks and quarries became the property of Guest, Keen & Nettlefolds Ltd. continuing in production until the closure

of the railway. Approaching the station, No. 2 signal box, again a lofty structure, was passed on the right before arriving at the compact station, just one platform with run-round facilities, four goods sidings and a single-road engine shed. The original shed blew down in a gale (some say it fell down of its own accord!) and the former LNWR shed in the vee of the junction was used until a replacement was built. This housed one or two tank engines for working the local traffic until closure in April 1960.

A major source of traffic to rail in later years was the chemical plant operated by ICI near Dowlais No. 1 Jct. Block tank trains of ammonia and methanol were operated to ICI Billingham, the Valley routes changing as lines were closed until the plant closed in 1965.

Dowlais Central Yard and Platform on 27 April 1960 when both passenger and freight traffic are in evidence. (E.T. Gill/ R.K. Blencowe Collection)

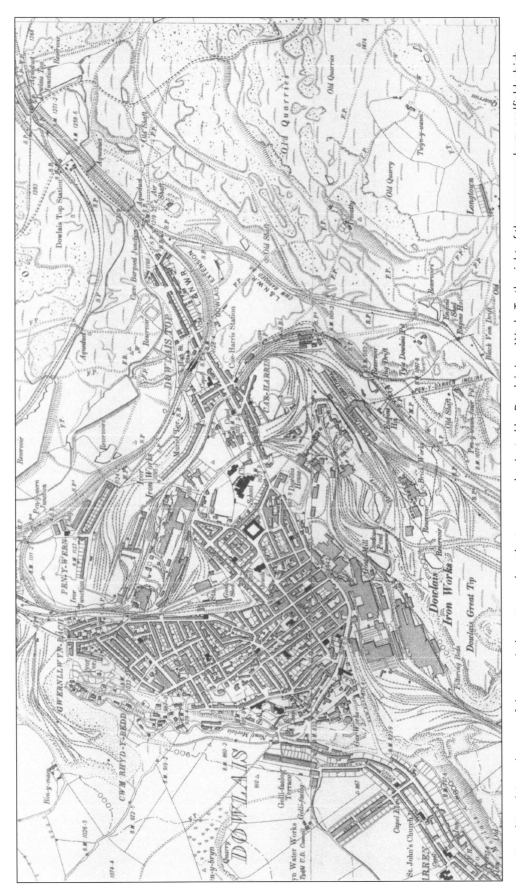

OS Map of Dowlais at the turn of the twentieth century, when the town was dominated by Dowlais Iron Works To the right of the map was a huge coalfield which did not survive the closure of the Ironworks in 1936, but has since been included in the Cwmbargoed Opencast development and currently Ffos-y-Fran. The town saw terrible poverty in the 1920s and '30s, and currently the inhabitants have been deprived of their railways, following the cutbacks of the 1960s. (National Library of Scotland)

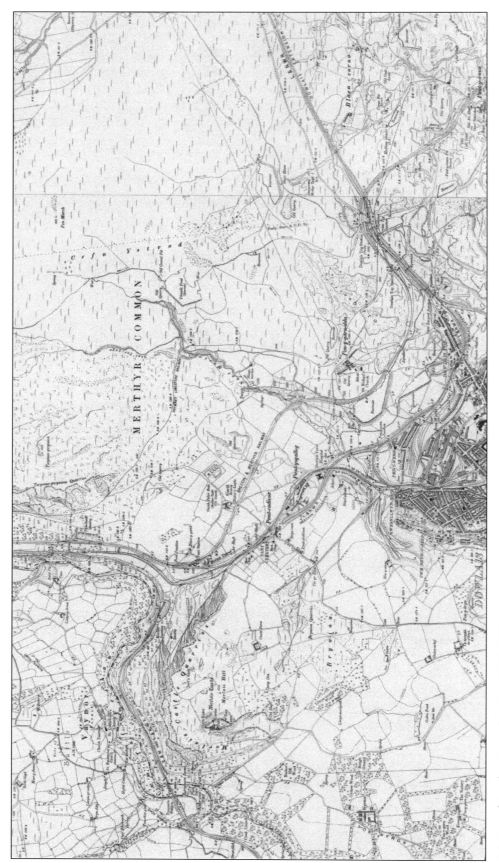

OS Map of Dowlais Central to Pant 1888-1913. (National Library of Scotland)

A view along the platform to the Goods Shed on 11 April 1964.
(Michael Roach)

Dowlais Central in the 1950s with the passenger platform and two-coach train, Goods Shed and Engine Shed in view.
(SLS)

A B&M Chair made at Machen Works at Dowlais central on 12 April 1964.
(R.O. Tuck)

Dowlais Central on 13 October 1962 with little evidence of traffic. The engine shed is extreme right. (W.G. Sumner)

Looking north from the passenger platform c1963. The passenger service had been withdrawn in May 1960. (Lens of Sutton)

Dowlais Lloyd Street in 1922, before renaming by the GWR to Dowlais Central with a passenger train waiting to depart which would be worked by an engine as in the next picture, probably the same engine. (D.K. Jones Collection)

Before the Grouping, the station was known as Dowlais Lloyd Street. This historic photograph shows B&M 18 being made ready for its last run in B&M service in 1922 at the shed. (LCGB Collection/NRM)

B&M 17 at the head of a departing goods service at Dowlais Lloyd Street c1922. To the left can be seen the Ivor Works of Guest, Keen & Nettlefolds which contributed much to the railway's freight traffic at that time. (LCGB Collection/NRM)

B&M 17 waiting to depart with a train to Pant, Pontsticill or Merthyr in c1922. Note there is passenger stock on the other side of the island platform. (LCGB /NRM)

The driver and fireman pose with B&M 0-6-0T No. 18 before working another service to Pant at the Grouping. (LCGB/NRM)

B&M 17 approaching Ivor Junction with the 3.50pm Dowlais Central to Pant service at the Grouping. (LCGB/NRM)

Dowlais Ivor Junction No. 1 SB where the tracks split between the B&M line to Pant to the left and the LNW line to the MT&A on the right. In the foreground, the Dowlais Works line crosses on the flat to the 'cinder tip', later the site of the ICI ammonia works. In the right background can be seen the remains of the LNWR engine shed. (D.K. Jones Collection)

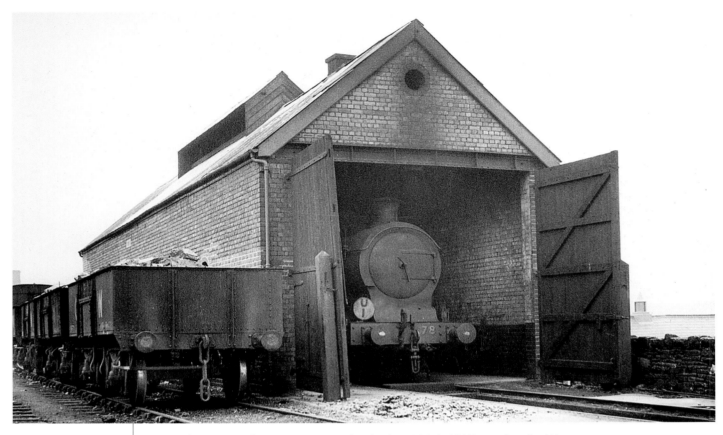

Former Rhymney Railway 78 occupies the shed on 21 July 1935 carrying the U1 target. (SLS)

4690 stands outside the small engine shed on 10 July 1958. (H.C. Casserley)

Another view of 333 with the 1.20pm to Pant on 29 March 1948. (W.A. Camwell/ SLS)

By the 1950s, the U1 passenger duty had often been passed to a 57XX as here with 5711 with the two coach train to Pant on 3 June 1950. (Ian L. Wright)

The 2.38pm Bargoed to Dowlais Central arriving on 10 July 1958, the engine having run round at Pant. (H.C. Casserley)

The same train having just arrived with Merthyr's 4632 on 27 April 1960. (E.T. Gill/R.K. Blencowe Collection)

A wider-angle perspective of the platform and yard showing the passenger island platform in use on both sides and several other wagons in the yard with 9676 awaiting departure with the passenger train to Pant on 6 May 1960. (E.T. Gill/R.K. Blencowe Collection)

An excellent view of TV 04 211 (previously 320) about to start the 2.45pm service to Pant on 24 March 1955. (W.A. Camwell/SLS)

Former Rhymney Railway Third Class Coach W1078 working the Dowlais-Pant service on 17 June 1951. (SLS)

Empty ammonia tanks often returned in small numbers routed via Merthyr rather than in the block train. In these two shots, they arrive back at Dowlais as part of a freight from Merthyr behind Merthyr's 4690 on 13 October 1962. (W.G. Sumner)

The final passenger train ever to use Dowlais Central was the SLS tour on 2 May 1964 from Merthyr to Brecon and back via Dowlais, powered by 3690 and 4555. The train is seen leaving the station en route back to Pontsticill where it would reverse and carry on to Merthyr.
(John Hodge)

The derelict Ivor Jct. No. 2 SB features in this shot of 4555 shunting the stock of the SLS Special ready for 3690 to attach front for departure to Pontsticill.
(John Hodge)

Dowlais Central still with the ammonia traffic passing on 4 August 1963. (Garth Tilt)

Dowlais Central after removal of all trackwork as seen on 15 October 1967. (Garth Tilt)

Passenger & Freight Working

The 1910 Bradshaw shows connections at Pant to Dowlais from the three main line Brecon trains in each direction. There was also at this period a 12 noon departure from Brecon which ran direct to Dowlais (Lloyd Street) and after a short layover returned to Brecon.

In the 1924 Service Timetable, the density of workings gives the impression that at least two engines were based at Dowlais Lloyd Street. Dowlais Turn D2 left at 5.50am to work light engine to Dowlais Top where it attached coaches and worked a workmen's train to Groesfaen Colliery, with appropriate stops along the way. The empty stock then ran on to Bargoed, whereupon D2 became a freight working to Pantywaun, then the freight marshalling concentration point on the B&M, and the main source of coal supply to Dowlais ironworks. Returning to Dowlais Top, it performed shunting there before working on to Pontsticill Jct. for more shunting around the limestone sidings and the reservoir extension then under construction, before returning to Dowlais for crew change at 1.34pm.

D2 then left Dowlais again at 2.30pm daily, again light to Dowlais Top for an hour's shunting in the clay sidings, another hour's shunting at Pontsticill, 25mins at Pantywaun, another 35mins at Pontsticill, before returning to Dowlais at 9.1pm precisely and another crew change.

Meanwhile, the daily passenger service from Dowlais amounted to seven journeys to Pant, three extended to Pontsticill on certain days, plus a MSO working. There was also a SO working at 9.15pm from Dowlais to Fleur-de-Lis, the return working arriving back at Dowlais at 11.5pm.

By 1938, there was a 5.12am working from Dowlais to Bedwas colliery, a miners' train reflecting the movement of colliers between pits due to the closure of pits in the Pantywaun area which had been decimated by the closure of Dowlais ironworks supplying collieries. The train called at Bargoed, Pengam (Mon), Fleur-de-Lis and Maesycwmmer, showing the extent of the miners affected. It returned from Bedwas at 7.28am bringing the Bedwas Colliery nightshift. This train was followed by another miners' train from Dowlais to Groesfaen at 5.20am which ran on empty to Bargoed and returned at 6.30am, collecting the night shift from Groesfaen. There were similar workings to and from Bedwas to suit the afternoon and night shift changeover times, the service providing also for the Groesfaen miners. In addition, there were seven passenger services daily to and from Pant.

The freight working at this date consisted of one duty for turn U2 (the target changed from D to avoid confusion with Cardiff East Dock who also worked to Dowlais with inter-works traffic from GKN Cardiff Docks). On SX, it left Dowlais Central at 4.46pm for Pontsticill, thence to Bargoed, back to Pontsticill and then back to Dowlais arriving at 8.45pm. Two new features in this timetable were a daily LMS freight arr.9.17am dep. 9.50am; also a ThO LMS cattle train, arr. 6.21am dep 6.50am, both of which would have used the connection from Penywern Jct.

The passenger service between Dowlais Central and Pant was withdrawn on 30 June 1952, though the miners' service workmen's trains continued as evidenced by the Winter 1954 Timetable and were said to have accommodated all-comers. The 5.2am workmen's train to Bargoed (for Groesfaen miners) was still running, as were the appropriate ones for shift changeovers and returns.

The freight workings in 1954 appeared to involve two engines from Dowlais Central, one leaving at 8am for Pontsticill, the other at 9.25am for Bargoed, though their subsequent workings are not available. Small pieces of information on U1 and U2 duties working from Pontsticill to Dowlais have survived but the whole is rather disjointed, as being subject to requirements. There were two former LMS workings, one from Nantybwch arr. 9.29am returning to Abergavenny Jct. at 9.49am, the other arriving from Abergavenny at 4.25pm dep. 5.25pm. Both were soon to cease with the closure of the Merthyr, Tredegar & Abergavenny route in January 1958.

Dowlais Iron Works

The works were founded as a partnership of nine in September 1759 with a capital of £4,000, though more importantly the right to mine iron ore, coal and limestone, plus a patented machine for blowing furnaces. In April 1767, John Guest was appointed manager and in 1786, he was succeeded by his son Thomas Guest who introduced many innovations to boost what had been a struggling concern previously. Thomas died in 1807 and was succeeded by his son John Josiah Guest, who became sole manager in 1815, owning nine of the sixteen shares in the works. Under Guest's leadership the works gained the reputation of being one of the world's great industrial concerns.

In 1821, the works supplied the tracks for the Stockton & Darlington Railway, the first ever passenger railway and over the next thirty years provided much of the track for the developing railways, with many foreign orders in the mid-1830s, such as for railways in Berlin, Leipzig and St Petersburg. At its peak in 1845, the works operated eighteen blast furnaces with a workforce of 7,300, producing over 88,000 tons of iron each year.

John Josiah Guest was knighted in 1838 and died in 1852, having become sole owner in 1851. Guest's widow Lady Charlotte was named as one of three executors and in 1855 married again to Henry Bruce who thus inherited control and was later to become Lord Aberdare. The works had been in decline for a while but Clark, the other executor, took rapid control of the situation, appointing William Menelaus as General Manager.

He introduced the Bessemer process there for conversion to making steel, but it took nine years for the system to be fully introduced, with working relations being developed with the Consett Iron Co. and Krupp. By 1857, Clark and Menelaus had constructed the Goat Mill, the world's most powerful rolling mill. With steel making being developed in many areas, there was a market slump and cash was very tight for new development; new financial accounting methods were introduced, leading to the present Cash Flow Statement. By the mid-1860s, Clark's reforms had borne fruit and the plant was showing renewed profitability. Clark delegated day to day management to Menelaus, but his trusteeship ended in 1864 when ownership passed to Sir Ivor Guest. Clark however continued to direct policy and built a new plant at Cardiff Docks to address the problem of having to carry imported iron ore from the port of Cardiff uphill to Dowlais. He retired in 1897 following which a major switch in the company was heralded.

More interested in other projects, Sir Ivor Guest sold the works to Arthur Keen in 1899 who formed Guest, Keen & Co. In 1902, Keen purchased Nettlefolds Ltd. to create Guest, Keen & Nettlefolds. Unlike the Merthyr Cyfarthfa Works, the early conversion to steel production allowed it to survive until the mid-1930s, but market conditions and competition from other South Wales and English plants alongside the Depression, caused the works to cease production at Dowlais in 1936 and concentrate their activities at Cardiff East Moors. However, the iron foundry and engineering works at Dowlais continued, known as the Ifor Works after John Josiah Guest's son Ifor, and new facilities were introduced there after 1945.

The Dowlais operation continued for several years as the Dowlais Foundry & Engineering Co. and became part of the nationalised British Steel Corporation in

1973 but closed in 1987 when the Cardiff plant took over its remaining business interests.

The Ivor Works was developed into a sulphate of ammonia plant in 1928, as part of a coke and by-products plant, including crude benzyl and tar. The controlling building was known as Ammonia House, Ifor Ironworks, Dowlais. The plant became the Dowlais Imperial Chemical Industries plant, owned by ICI, opening in 1938, the site chosen with other factories as potentially safe from air attack and suitable because of the availability of manpower, supplies of soft water and raw materials. The factory continued to expand in the 1940s and early 1950s when a flow of ammonia for use in the manufacture of explosives and fertilisers began to ICI Billingham in tank wagons, consigned in trainloads, lasting until the factory closed in 1963. The traffic initially passed via Talyllyn East Jct. and on to Hereford, but when this route was closed in December 1962, it ran down the Valley to Maesycwmmer Jct. and on to Pontypool Road. In early days the train was hauled by a 2301 Class 0-6-0, but in the 1950s, this gave way to a Merthyr 56XX, suitably assisted, as far as Hereford, then by a pair of Merthyr 57XX, and finally by a Pontypool Road 56XX when the route south from Pant was followed.

A painting of the Dowlais Ironworks in full flow. (Ken Mumford Presentations)

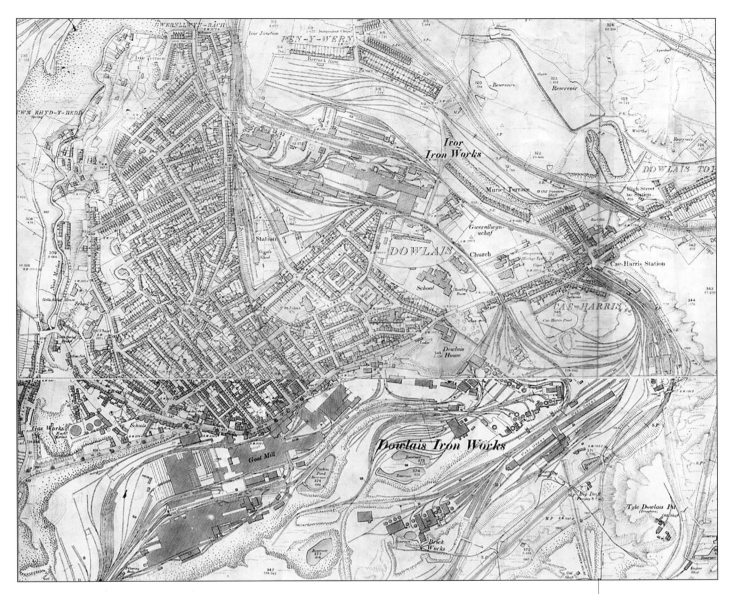

A map of Dowlais
Iron Works.
(Ken Mumford Presentations)

Dowlais Works
sidings. (Merthyr Library)

Dowlais Works in the 1930s. (Merthyr Library)

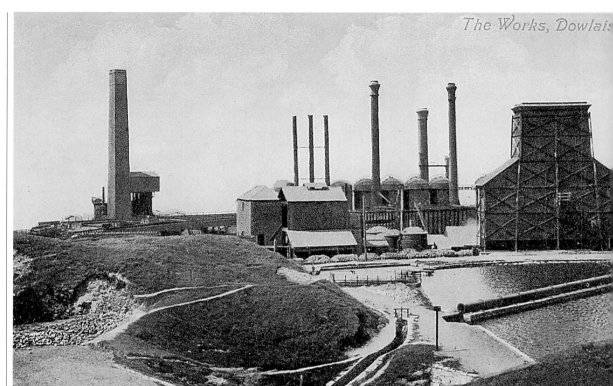

Dowlais Works Works engines renamed on occasion of Royal visit to works.